Thanksgiving

The **power** to **transform** your life

Book Three

A daily devotional to bring you into the presence of God

Stella Doggett

Published by
The Centre for Life Management
172 Long Street,
Dordon, England.
B78 1QA
www.lifetraining.co.uk,

Copyright © Stella Doggett 2023

Unless otherwise indicated all scripture quotations are taken from the New International Version, Copyright © 1978 New York International Bible Society, published in the UK by Hodder & Stoughton.

RSV. Revised Standard Version, Copyright © 1946,1952 The division of Christian education of the national council of the churches of Christ in the USA.

AMP. The Amplified Bible, Expanded Edition Copyright © 1987 Zondervan Corporation and The Lockman Foundation.

TPT. The Passion Translation, New Testament with Psalms, Proverbs, and Song of Songs Copyright © 2018 Broadstreet Publishing group, LLC

NASB. New American Standard Bible Copyright © 1995 The Lockman Foundation.

The Message. Copyright © 2004 by Eugene H. Peterson.

AV. King James Authorised Version.

ISBN 978-1-7392333-2-7

Cover design by Sian James cre8sian_art@yahoo.com
Typeset by Angela Selfe
Project managed by theweddedhare@gmail.com

Acknowledgements

I would like to thank all those who have helped me to complete this third book including those who have sent me their encouraging feedback from Books One and Two.

Once again my wonderful and patient husband Mark, my 'joint heir of the grace of life', (1 Peter 3:7, AMP.) has faithfully and patiently encouraged me, edited, and checked both the biblical references and context of these daily readings. He has also written several of the daily reflections himself. Your support, practical and spiritual, has been amazing and yet again I have to say that without your company on our journey of life with Jesus, these readings would have been far less rich and may never have seen the light of day.

Thanks also to our fellowship group here in Dordon who have prayed for me and cheered me on. Thanks again to John who has continued to faithfully 'proof read' each of the 'Days', and to Bridget who has joined the proof reading team. In any biblical quotations that I have written out, all use of bold print indicates my emphasis and is not as printed in the original publication.

Introduction

Those of you who have read Books One and Two, covering the first six months of the year, will be familiar with the story behind the writing of these books but I will repeat some of it because I believe it is so important that you know why these daily readings have been written and are now published for you to read.

I believe that the Lord said that in these days He is wanting to release a spirit of gratitude over His people. He wants to shift the mindset of His followers to embrace gratitude as a lifestyle. It seemed that the Lord was saying to me that if I would write it down, He would give me a message on 'Thanksgiving' for every day for a year. And He did!

The Lord is, I believe, positioning us, His people, to live above the chaos of the world at this time, and to instead be 'light' in the darkness. Now is 'our turn to shine' (Isaiah 60:1,2). As the Lord, in the coming days, months and years, pours His grace upon His people I pray that these daily readings will help to prepare your heart to receive that grace in order that you will grow stronger and shine brighter than ever day by day.

The readings are not about listing 365 things for which we can be thankful, because there are many, many more than 365 of those. They are about the power of thanksgiving in our lives; about the transformation thanksgiving works in us and for us, as it feeds our hearts with God's truth, draws us into His grace and love, builds our faith and bring us into an awareness of His presence. At the core they are about becoming so aware, grateful and thankful to Him for all He is, and all that He does for us.

This book, Book Three, now covers the third quarter of the year and on some of the days you will notice some reoccurring themes. Like the children of Israel we often have to revisit familiar truths in order to remind ourselves of the ground on which we stand, and of the momentous truths which sit at the heart of our wonderful Salvation story. My intention is that truths revisited will come through these pages with fresh light and in a new way – less we forget!!!

On other days you will find completely new thoughts and suggestions, and my prayer is that as you continue this journey of 'Thanksgiving' you will find your relationship with the Almighty and hence the whole of your life, being increasingly enriched both spiritually and naturally.

As before on each day you will find a suggested activation. Personalising these suggestions will help you to be a 'doer' of the word and not just a 'hearer', (James 1:23). So please use these reflections in your own way, and let the Holy Spirit bless you and fill you as you 'Enter His Gates' and find Him to be all that you need.

Enjoy!!

DAY 183 | Thanksgiving to Start Every Day

If you have read through Books One and Two you will now have been on our journey of thanksgiving for six months, and it struck me that we can summarise some of the things that the Lord has been teaching us very simply.

Firstly thanksgiving creates a relational connection with our God, (and also with other people), like nothing else. Remember how in Romans 1:21 Paul explains that a failure to give God thanks was a large part of the start of the downfall of man. If a lack of thanksgiving is what separated humankind from the Lord, how much more will a heart of thanksgiving daily draw us closer to Him. Thanksgiving in all our circumstances will stop the enemy from sowing those seeds of doubt and unbelief into our hearts and minds that can result in us feeling separated from the Lord and His relentless love.

Secondly thanksgiving connects our spirit to God's goodness like nothing else. We read in Amos 3:3 God's rhetorical question to the Israelites, "Can two walk together, except they be agreed?" (AV). Well obviously the answer to that question is 'no', and we have seen the power that thanksgiving has to bring us into our own agreement with God; that He is good, that He is for us, that He is with us throughout each and every day and in every circumstance, and that He will work in everything for our good to make us more like Jesus day by day. (Romans 8:28,29).

I believe therefore that, through this journey we are on, the Lord is creating a mindset in us so that we start each and every day with 'Thank You'. First of all, 'Thank you for the gift of this new day' – A whole day ahead in which to walk with Jesus, and talk with Him and learn from Him, so that like the Psalmist we can start the day saying, "This is the day the Lord has made; let us rejoice and be glad in it." (Psalm 118:24).

Then we can thank Him for the new mercies, new love, and new faithfulness stored up for us and ready to be poured out upon us throughout the day. 'Because of the Lord's great love we are not consumed, for His compassions never fail, they are new every morning; great is your faithfulness.'

(Lamentations 3:22,23). We can thank Him that there will be forgiveness for every mistake we make throughout the day, and for every sin we commit.

Next we can thank Him that He will be present with us throughout the day, however the day is going to pan out. His name is Emmanuel, 'God with us', and furthermore God has said, "Never will I leave you; never will I forsake you." (Hebrews 13:5). In the Amplified Bible the footnote tells us that there is something of a triple negative before the verb here, so it can read 'I will not, I will not, I will not forsake you'. (Which is worth meditating on in case you were in any doubt!)

We can then thank Him for the provision for all that this new day holds. He is not going to be surprised at anything that comes at us. We can thank Him that 'The Lord is my shepherd, I shall not be in want.' (Psalm 23:1), and that today there will be grace for everything. 'And God is able to make all grace abound to you, so that in all things at all times, having all that you need, you will abound in every good work.' (2 Corinthians 9:8). Just pause and look at those words **'all** and **every**.' Thank Him that there is already grace stored up for every challenge.

Finally, (may be?) we can thank Him for all the opportunities to shed abroad His love into the lives of the people that we are going to meet in this day. I believe as we come to Him in the morning we can be like the Amazon delivery person, loading ourselves up with the Lord's goodness, kindness, healing, encouragements and gifts ready to distribute throughout the day to those we meet.

Activation ...

As you choose to start your day with these 'Thank Yous' you become open to receive all that He has for you. Thanksgiving for the day, at the start of the day, is part of you receiving all that you need for the day, enabling you to walk more in step with Him and to become more like Him in every way.

DAY 184 | Overflowing with Thanksgiving

'"Further up and further in." cried Jewel and instantly they were off again.' Those of you who have enjoyed the Narnia books of C.S. Lewis will recognise this cry from the last chapter of 'The Last Battle'. It seems to me it could echo Paul's heart as he wrote to his friends in Philippi; 'But one thing I do: Forgetting what is behind and straining toward what is ahead, I press on toward the goal to win the prize for which God has called me heavenward in Jesus Christ.' (Philippians 3:13,14).

So what has that to do with thanksgiving? Well, I was recently reading Colossians 2:6,7, 'So then, just as you received Christ Jesus as Lord, continue to live in Him, rooted and built up in Him, strengthened in the faith as you were taught, and **overflowing with thankfulness**.' It seemed to me that, as we start the second half of our year of thanksgiving with this book (Book 3), it is worth reflecting on this encouragement to overflow with thankfulness, and how this can help us to 'press on' in our life of faith without feeling that we are pushing ourselves in an uncomfortable or driven way.

As new or young Christians, we are often naturally full of gratitude, knowing that Jesus has saved and forgiven us. We can be overflowing with it. Then, as we get older, more 'sophisticated and respectable', we can still believe the truth but be less excited by it. We can even loose that joy expressed in the song written by Mick Ray many years ago … "I get so excited Lord every time I realise; I'm forgiven, I'm forgiven."

We may be tempted to say, "I have moved on to the deeper things of God." Fine, but if you or I are no longer getting, 'so excited that Jesus has done it all', and that we are completely forgiven, then perhaps we need to have a look at Revelation 2:4. This is Jesus' letter to the persevering church in Ephesus, who had 'forsaken their first love'. It shows us that God's desire is for a people who don't 'cool off' in their love as time goes by. So how do we keep 'our first love', and press on in our journey of faith with joy in our hearts?

It is said 'beauty is in the eye of the beholder' and, if so, then we need to keep our eyes fastened on Jesus (Hebrews 12:2) and see what happens! His beauty will cause us to love Him more and more as time goes by, and I think that, over the last six months, we have seen that thanksgiving is one of the best ways to keep our eyes, heart, mind and emotions fixed on Jesus.

Wonderfully, it is a two way process. We keep our eyes on Him and joy wells up from deep within, from our spirit. Thanksgiving arises for who He is and what He has done for us and so it helps us to keep drawing fresh water from the wells of salvation. (See Isaiah 12:3). This is not about beating yourself up by saying, 'I must be more thankful', this is about soaking yourself in the Lord, His word, His promises, His goodness, what He has done, and in prayers answered.

As we look at all these things, gratitude springs up in our hearts and the water of life bubbles up more and more strongly till it overflows, alongside our thanksgiving. Now this is not an extraverts' charter into which introverts have to squeeze themselves! Overflowing with thanksgiving doesn't have to be noisy, although it can be, like the 'walking and jumping and praising God.' of Acts 3:8. Joy and thanksgiving can also be evident in our lives as a quiet radiance, 'those who look to him are radiant:' (Psalm 34:5). So however we express it, let's look for a strong river that overflows, whether in an 'explosive' burst, or a strong, deepening, persistent flow.

Finally, the word 'habits' can get a bad name, but good ones (like brushing your teeth) can do wonders for your health. The more deeply thanksgiving is embedded in the flow of my life, the more it will become second nature and a 'good habit'. It will be of great benefit to me, and to those around me who will get wet in the overflow, and of course it will greatly bless the Lord Jesus, who along with the Father and the Spirit deserve all the genuine gratitude that we can give.

Activation ...

At the beginning of this next three months of our 'Thanksgiving Journey', resolve again to make your life one of 'Thanksgiving'. Noisy or quiet it can be fun. Receive much joy from the Lord as you give thanks and draw from those deep wells of salvation. With God there is always more, and so living with an overflow of thanksgiving will help you to live out of the wonderful flow of **life** that Jesus offers you daily.

DAY 185 | Thanksgiving for Transformation not Conformity

We have frequently talked in these meditations about the fact that God has 'decided' to make us like Jesus. He has predestined us to be, 'conformed to the likeness of His Son, that he might be the firstborn among many brothers.' This is wonderful since we also know that God is for us ... and will along with Christ 'graciously give us all things'. This is the cause of much of our thanksgiving because this plan God has, to make us like Jesus, is linked to those promises that, 'in all things God works for the good of those who love him,' and that 'nothing will be able to separate us from the love of God that is in Christ Jesus our Lord.' (Romans 8:28-39).

When Mark, my husband, was at school they had a certain master who would frequently tell the boys, "You must conform". So the first thing that comes to mind today, with regards to thanksgiving, is that as He transforms me into the image of His Son, God does not demand 'conformity'. He has created us all as totally unique and wonderful beings. His plan is that through each of us – individuals that we are – the Glory of His person and His character would shine in a unique but recognisable way.

In 2021 we were watching the news coverage of the 100th anniversary celebrations of the Communist Party of China, and observing the incredible precision and uniformity of all the participants, even to the fixed smiles and movements of the dancers. It was uniformity and conformity in the extreme. It was quite chilling in what it portrayed of the power of the regime, and there at the front stood the supreme leader, rigid and straight faced, in grey, surrounded by his security guards.

In my mind's eye I couldn't help but contrast that with the picture I have of heaven; the beauty and spontaneity of the angelic worship, and the immense variety of people we will see worshipping God when we get there. So many, many different ones all reflecting, in their own way, the glory of the King. So firstly let us thank the Lord that our transformation into His likeness is not being imposed upon us by threats or external force, but by something truly amazing – the power of the Holy Spirit working in and with our spirit.

I am just so thankful that God is not an autocrat compelling me to behave 'clone like' in exactly the same way as all other Christians. There is also no heavy duty laid upon me that I must modify my behavior until I reach the right standard. Instead, while we are still on earth the encouragement to us is not to conform to the patterns that we see all around us but to be transformed by the renewing of our minds. (Romans 12:2).

If we aren't truly amazed by all this grace, we are missing something. We are saved by grace and we are being transformed by His grace. The Holy Spirit is helping us day by day to live out our lives from our 'new self' in Christ, as described by the apostle Paul in his letter to the Galatians. The Holy Spirit is helping us to choose to live from our spirit and to put off the old self and his/her ways, 'that you be renewed in the spirit of your mind, and put on the new self, which in *the likeness of* God has been created in righteousness and holiness of the truth.' (Ephesians 4:22-24 NASB).

Activation...

As you grasp again the immensity of this salvation, your gratitude and thanksgiving can only help to speed your cooperation and therefore your transformation.

Giving thanks for the wonderful work of the Holy Spirit in your life is like saying, 'O Lord, you are our Father. We are the clay, you are the potter; we are all the work of your hand.' (Isaiah 64:8).

DAY 186 | Thanksgiving that we are Being Transformed

Yesterday, we were rejoicing that in the Kingdom of God 'transformation' – 'being conformed to the likeness of God's Son', (Romans 8:29) – is not a kind of spiritual 'cloning' that will leave us all looking and talking alike. That is not in God's plan. God's creation is full of spectacular variety, and His new creation is no different.

The transformation that is taking place in our lives – once we have become Christians – is just amazing because it means that one day we are going to look like Jesus in His character and beauty. Let's consider again Paul's words to the Corinthian church. 'But we all, with unveiled face, beholding as in a mirror the glory of the Lord, **are being transformed into the same image from glory to glory**, just as from the Lord, the Spirit.' (2 Corinthians 3:18. NASB).

No one knows what Jesus looked like or exactly how He walked or talked, and I'm glad. We are not called to mimic Him. We do however know what He said and what He did, and we see His beauty in all His dealings with the people He met while He was on the earth. Being transformed into the image of God's Son must therefore be the most wonderful destiny any of us on earth can have. There is never any need for any of us to say I have no purpose or meaning. We are destined to carry His image in ever increasing glory throughout this life, and on into eternity. Now that is some calling; one for which I can and will be eternally grateful.

A second thing that I am so, so grateful about today, is that you and I have not joined a 'self improvement' society. It's not about me pulling myself up by my boot straps, it is all about grace and the work of our beautiful helper the Holy Spirit. This transformation is 'from the Lord, the Spirit.' As we look at Jesus, it's like looking in a glass showing us the future 'us'. Incredible as it seems, that is what we are going to look like when He returns and we see Him face to face, (1 John 3:2), and although we are totally part of this transformation process, it is not, thankfully, down to my will power, or self effort to change.

Transformation happens through the enlightenment and revelation that the Holy Spirit brings, as He

i) tells us who we now are in Christ – children of our heavenly Father who lavishes His love upon us. (1 John 3:1),

ii) shows us how much we are loved – the breadth, length, height and depth of all that love. (Ephesians 3:17-19), and as He

iii) refreshes, restores, and corrects us and leads us into paths of righteousness, 'for His names sake'. (Psalm 23:2,3), and

iv) prays for us and within us when we have no words or understanding. (Romans 8:26)...

and so much more.

Activation...

Thank the Holy Spirit today for being your on board Helper. The one who is intent on helping you to fulfill your wonderful destiny of becoming like Jesus.

Thank Him that, as He helps you on this journey of transformation, there is no coercion only love.

You could also write down here – adding to the list above – some of those other ways in which He helps you, and give Him thanks for those also.

DAY 187 | Thanksgiving for Abundant Grace

Yesterday we were looking at the 'amazing grace' of which we are recipients, not just the one off event when I was born again, but the amazing grace which is transforming me day by day. As in John Newton's wonderful hymn, there is the 'Amazing grace that saved a wretch like me' – and there is the grace 'that brought me safe thus far', and the grace 'that will lead me home'.

Today's thought is a simple one but it's just so profound, and I hope it will provoke some of that overflowing gratitude in your heart, and on your lips. It is simply this; **that this 'Amazing Grace' will never ever run out**. Sometimes we hear about shortages of different items coming into our stores. Then the fear that some essential, (and not so essential), things might run out and disappear from the shelves in our shops causes people to buy far more than they could use of various items. We call it stockpiling.

Fear does that to you. You have to hoard and protect yourself from possible future lack. Well today let us thank God that there is **an abundance of grace**. There is no need to stockpile, and you can't stockpile grace even if you wanted to, it's a moment by moment thing. It's about walking with the Lord day by day, hour by hour, rather than storing it up. I wonder if this is why the 'big meeting euphoria' only lasts a little while, if we don't take what we have learnt and feed it to ourselves daily.

We can't store up grace because the Christian life is about 'walking' with the Lord in friendship and relationship, it is not about 'charging ourselves up' as if we were a phone or an ipad. There is however, always grace available when we need it. Corrie Ten Boom recalls how her father answered her question about how she might handle future events like death or suffering. He replied by saying that in the same way that he would give her the ticket for her train journey when they reached the station, even so God would give her the grace that she needed when the time came.

This is why there is no point in worrying about how you will cope with tomorrow's challenges because you are anticipating them without tomorrow's grace to handle them. That will come tomorrow when it is needed. In Jesus words, "So do not worry about tomorrow; for tomorrow will care for itself. Each day has enough trouble of its own" (Matthew 6:34, NASB).

Whether it is grace to handle the challenges of the day, or the grace that we need constantly at work in our lives to transform us into the likeness of Jesus, the truth is that our 'God is able to make all grace abound to you, so that in all things at all times, having all that you need, you will abound in every good work.' (2 Corinthians 9:8).

Activation ...

Give thanks today firstly that there is an **abundance of grace**. Grace that has saved us and grace that is working transformation in us as life unfolds day by day. Remind yourself as you give thanks that it is never ever going to run out.

Secondly give thanks that the grace you are going to need, moment by moment, to meet the various challenges that every day brings, is also freely available to you by His Spirit, in a never ending flow.

And finally give thanks that there will be grace for tomorrow, whatever it brings. We can't, and nor is there any need to, 'stockpile'. The Holy Spirit is our never failing Helper who loves to keep us walking closely with the Lord, as we receive all the grace He imparts to us, moment by moment.

DAY 188 | The Ladder of Thanksgiving

Today we are looking at the amazing statement that Jesus made as He encouraged His disciples to exercise their faith. He said, "I tell you the truth, if you have faith as small as a mustard seed, you can say to this mountain, 'move from here to there', and it will move. **Nothing will be impossible for you."** (Matthew 17:20). It was an encouragement, but if not heard correctly it can lead to a journey of introspection as we look inwards to see if that 'mustard seed of faith' is there in our hearts. This of course can lead to discouragement.

The thing about the people who came to Jesus and 'got' their 'impossibility' was that they weren't looking at themselves but at Jesus. They knew, "If I just touch His clothes, I will be healed." (Mark 5:28), or for the centurion it was, "But say the word, and my servant will be healed." (Luke 7:7). For Bartimaeus it was, 'If I can just get His attention and can tell Him, "Rabbi, I want to see." I will gain my sight.' (Mark 10:51). They knew all the power was His and they just had to get close enough to catch His eye and put their case. That was their part. Their faith was expressed by their reaching out to 'touch' Him in some way, the miracle was His to bring about.

All those who experienced a miracle in the gospel narrative, came to Jesus because they 'saw' that things changed when He was around. They came because they heard about the miracles others had experienced, and they came because they had no other means of seeing their condition change. The fact is that this 'grain of mustard seed' faith, is not about what's going on inside me, but about who I see Jesus to be for me in the situation. If I see Him as, 'the God who gives life to the dead and calls things that are not as though they were.' (Romans 4:17), then I am half way to having my miracle; to seeing my 'impossibility' become possible.

When we are facing an impossibility and we look at our faith levels, it can be as if we are at the bottom of a deep pit with vertical sides. We can feel as if we should be at the top of those steep sides – full of faith – if we are going to see our 'impossibility' become a reality. The vertical climb up to that level of faith looks impossible in itself, but this is where the wonderful ladder of thanksgiving can help us climb.

Let us imagine that this ladder reaches from the bottom of the pit to the top. The bottom of the pit represents total unbelief, and the top fullness of faith. Then imagine that each rung of the ladder is something which the Lord has done for us, or for others, for which we can thank him. In this way our own testimony, and that of others, becomes the way in which our faith increases and we journey from 'unbelief' to 'faith'.

The thing about climbing a ladder to get out of a pit, is that you have to go up one rung at a time. We could get discouraged after we have stepped onto the first rung because it doesn't seem to have raised us very far, but unless we step on the first rung we will not be in a position to reach the second rung, and then the third etc. On and on up we go, one rung at a time, until we reach the top and can step out into the sunlight again, and onto firm ground.

Surely 'Blind Bartimaeus' had faith as 'a grain of mustard seed' because he had heard and recalled some stories of the miracles that others had experienced, and that propelled him to shout out for Jesus, persisting and creating that stir, until he got his healing. Choosing to intentionally give thanks for each and every miracle, or intervention of God in our lives, will enable us to fix our eyes on Jesus our friend, and all that He has done for us. We will be growing in faith step by step, rung by rung, for all that we need Him to do for us for our next miracle.

Abraham we are told, 'did not waver through unbelief regarding the promise of God, but was strengthened in faith and gave glory to God, **being fully persuaded that God had power to do what he had promised.**' (Romans 4:20,21). I think I'm with Abraham in this. I will give God all the glory I can when I see, or remember a miracle (however 'small'), and I will use it as a rung on my ladder, as I fix my eyes on Jesus and grow in faith for the next one.

Activation ...

Is there something that you need a grain of mustard seed faith for today? Start to climb that ladder of faith with thanksgiving for the things that you have seen God do for you or others, in the past, or that you have read about. Give God the glory for those things and let your faith rise as you do.

DAY 189 | The Breadth of Thanksgiving

Last week we were reflecting on the thought that the Lord is inviting us to overflow with thankfulness and gratitude (Colossians 2:7), and we considered how this could take the form of a bubbling spring welling up, or perhaps the quieter strong flow of a deep river. Those two pictures – of a gushing spring or a deep, strongly flowing river are both mainly two dimensional – they have depth and height and forward movement and they are wonderful pictures of overflowing thanksgiving. Now, as we read on in Colossians 3:17, more treasures emerge on this wonderful theme of 'overflowing with thanksgiving'.

The Holy Spirit is now inspiring us to expand our vision of thanksgiving as we read, 'And whatever you do, whether in word or deed, do it all in the name of the Lord Jesus, giving thanks to God the Father through him.' So there we have it, 'whatever you do, whether in word or deed' – whether it's something you **do** or something you **say**, – the Holy Spirit is inviting us to be thankful in everything we are **doing** and everything we are **saying**.

That doesn't leave much room for exceptions – even changing the baby's nappy, going to the shops, driving to work, or phoning the school about your child. It's all included! So the heart of God for our lives expands to be a totally 3D experience of thankfulness, not only with depth and flow, but also in the breadth of everything I do and say in my daily life. Nothing is too trivial, nothing too embarrassing, too human, too secular, too natural, too normal, or too everyday to not do, or say, with gratitude and thanksgiving.

This is a wonderful way of sanctifying the whole of life, so that there is no secular or sacred divide. We are temples of the Holy Spirit and therefore we are holy (set apart) and what we do and say needs to be seen as holy also. The key that helps us to unlock this mystery is found in the words **'do it all in the name of the Lord Jesus, giving thanks to God the Father through him.'** This then also links into our understanding of what it really means to pray 'in the name of the Lord Jesus'.

In Book 2, Day 158, we saw that praying in Jesus' name is very powerful. This is because if I come to the Father praying 'in Jesus name' I am presenting myself, with my request, before the Father as I stand in His righteousness. He has saved me and I now come before the Father, asking for the things that Jesus would be asking for, so that I can do the things on earth that He would do, and bear much fruit because I am 'abiding' or 'remaining' in Him.

So here's the thing; the Holy Spirit is on hand to enable us to overflow in thanksgiving in all areas of life, big and small, all our saying and doing, because God's desire, intention and grace towards us is that we can do all these things, and not just our praying, in the name of the Lord Jesus. We can draw on who He specifically is to us, and for us, in the whole of life, and that is so whether it's something big or small that I am doing, spiritual or natural, routine or unexpected, mundane or exciting, producing plentiful fruit or no obvious fruit.

This is linked to a breadth of understanding and vision that we don't just pray in Jesus' name for healing, for financial need, for family stresses, for help at work, or for spiritual battles – big stuff – but we bring Jesus' name, and that means 'who Jesus is', into everything we do and say, including the little things, the routine, the mundane, and all the things that demand our attention day by day. And we do that as we **'do it all in the name of the Lord Jesus, giving thanks to God the Father through him.'** We can see that there is a breadth to our thanksgiving, as we speak it out, in whatever we do or say, from the trivial, the daily routine, to today's big challenge.

Activation ...

Ask the Holy Spirit to show you just how involved the Lord is in all parts of your everyday life and conversations, how much everything can be done in Jesus' name as you give thanks for His indwelling presence that is with you in all that you do and say. Today let that broadness of gratitude and thankfulness well up and overflow. Or could it be the other way round? Chicken or egg? As you overflow in thanksgiving in every little or big thing that you do and say in your daily life, could it be that you will find, to your joy and amazement, that the Lord Jesus is involved with you in it all; in everything. No more "I couldn't bother you with that Lord." but rather a joyful, thankful engaging with Him throughout the whole of your life!

DAY 190 | Thanksgiving for 'Mercy and Majesty'

We know from Romans 5:20,21, that grace trumps sin, any time, and anywhere. In fact the revelation of grace in the early church was so powerful that Paul had to ask the question, 'Shall we go on sinning that grace may abound?' The answer was of course, 'By no means! We died to sin; how can we live in it any longer?' (Romans 6:1,2). Paul lived expecting and praying for the Christians to become more and more like Jesus, carrying His presence wherever they went.

This truth, that abundant grace is available to help us to grow and become more like Jesus can, however, risk us slipping into a kind of perfectionism with ourselves and others, as we seek to live out our new life in Christ. As we, through the power of the Holy Spirit working in us, look to produce the precious fruit described in Galatians 5:22,23, we also need to understand that we will still be needing the grace and forgiveness of God until the day we die and are completely transformed into His likeness. (1 John 3:2).

The 'Majesty' and 'Magnificence' of our King should not lead us to be afraid to bring Him our failures and weaknesses. We don't have to hide the bits of us that might cause us to feel ashamed. This is so different to the world where, the more important and powerful we see a person to be, the more we 'clean up' and 'hide' any weakness from them, particularly anything about us of which we feel they might be disapproving.

Let us, if we can, imagine a servant going before a medieval king or, in our day, an employee being called before the company director, or somebody with power, someone who can profoundly affect their future career. We know, if that was us, that we would smarten up and definitely hide any mistakes or failings. God, on the other hand, who has such a high calling for us and such incredible plans to share His glory with us, God who is the Mightiest and most Magnificent Being ever by such a long, long way, is also the safest place to reveal our weaknesses. In fact He wants us to bring them to Him – all of them – and to hide nothing.

I first learnt this lesson many years ago, when after a very difficult year of trying to be a 'good' and 'happy' and 'fruitful' Christian, I found myself feeling very low, and quite the failure in many areas of life. In church one Sunday the reading was of the man with the withered hand who Jesus healed in the synagogue. Jesus 'said to the man, "stretch out your hand". So he stretched it out and it was completely restored, just as sound as the other.' (Matthew 12:13).

It felt like the Lord was saying to me that I'd been trying so hard to be 'a good Christian', to be what I believed I should be but wasn't, and that I would always put out, or 'show', my good hand – what I perceived as my strengths – so much so that I never brought my 'withered parts' to Him but hid them. He helped me to see, through that passage, that I would try to always show Him (and my fellow Christians) my best parts, not the 'withered parts' because I feared that if He, or they, saw my weaknesses or failures, I would not be acceptable.

The wonderful truth that He taught me that day, and that I often have to revisit, is that not only am I a sinner saved by grace, which involved taking my sin to the cross, but that the journey towards being transformed to be like Him, also involves taking my weaknesses and failures to the cross, where they now belong, not hiding them or trying to sort them myself. It's about unconditional love and acceptance, not performance, and it's about bringing things into the light where the Lord can heal as we 'stretch out our withered hands'.

Activation ...

Thank Him today for the wonderful combination of Majesty and Mercy that there is in our King, a combination rarely found in the world. As you grasp the power of this combination to bring change, and restoration into your life, give thanks, and come 'boldly unto the throne of grace, . . . to obtain mercy and find grace to help in time of need'. (Hebrews 4:16 AV). Thanksgiving will also help you to resist the whispers of the enemy, inciting you to hide your weaknesses. This is so important because what you (think you can) hide from Him, you will also keep.

DAY 191 | Thanksgiving and Strength

In Isaiah 40:31 (AV) we read that wonderful promise, 'Those who wait upon the Lord will renew their strength; they shall mount up with wings as eagles; they shall run, and not be weary; they shall walk, and not faint.' In the passage those who do this 'waiting on the Lord' are contrasted with youths and young men – the ones that naturally have the most strength and resilience of us all – who may faint and fall by comparison. It is a wonderful promise to 'those who are tired and weary or feeling weak', and many of us could often put up our hands and say "That's me!", "Include me in that!", "I'd like some of that too!"

The difficulty can be however, that we read promises like these, and even claim them, and then wander off, and carry on living life as normal, and we wonder why the promise hasn't really been fulfilled. The reason for this is often down to a lack of understanding about this activity called 'waiting'.

As a child waiting always felt like a waste of time, after all who wants to wait until after Christmas lunch to have their presents!? Waiting in our current 'instant' society has always had a bit of a bad press, especially with fast food and next day deliveries now the norm. For many of us 'waiting' feels like a non-productive time, endured before something good happens.

In some situations, waiting can actually be quite a wearisome thing in itself. How many of us spend our 'waiting times' fretting because it feels like time is passing and absolutely nothing seems to be happening. Or we can wait and 'worry' that the thing that we want to happen, just won't. Either way, far from renewing our strength we can find waiting is energy sapping, but Isaiah is of course talking of a different kind of waiting, and it is that beautiful phrase 'upon the Lord' that makes all the difference.

In Psalm 123:2 (AV.) we read , 'as the eyes of a servant look unto the hand of their masters , and as the hand of a maiden unto the hand of her mistress; so our eyes wait upon the Lord our God, until He have mercy upon us.'. The Psalmist is in trouble, he is expecting deliverance from the Lord, and he shows that by using that word '**until**'. Although he doesn't know the exact time frame, he knows that God will come through for him.

This is a kind of waiting that is expectant, hopeful, and in fact the NIV translates the verse in Isaiah as, 'those who **hope** in the Lord will renew their strength'. This kind of waiting is about where our focus of attention is. Is it on the clock or the calendar, on the time that is passing, or on the Lord who made heaven and earth and who loves us so much? 'We wait in hope for the Lord; he is our help and our shield. In him our hearts rejoice, for we trust in his holy name. May your unfailing love rest upon us, O Lord, even as we put our trust in you.' (Psalm 33:20-22).

So here we find our connection to thanksgiving. When I am feeling tired and weary, it can just be physical, but I think that the kind of weariness that Isaiah speaks of here is probably connected to a feeling of discouragement too. In the previous verses to the promise that we are looking at, Isaiah asks the people of Israel, 'Why do you say, O Jacob, and complain, O Israel, "My way is hidden from the Lord; my cause is disregarded by my God"? He then reminds them of the fact that not only is their God the creator and sustainer of the earth but that He also has unfathomable understanding of them. (verse 28).

So if some, or even all, of our weariness is because we are feeling discouraged or even abandoned by God, let us turn our hearts in thanksgiving again for who He is and what He does. Waiting involves a passage of time, and our thanksgiving will slow us down and help us to take **enough time** to look at our God afresh, **enough time** to take in His love, His encouragements, His promises, and feed on these things rather than our circumstances or situation, remembering that we don't 'live on bread alone, but on every word that comes from the mouth of God'. (Matthew 4:4).

Activation ...

Let your thanksgiving today give you the time to truly 'wait on the Lord'; to have a good feed on His words and His character, and to renew your strength with His love.

DAY 192 | Thanksgiving and Renewing My Strength

Yesterday we wrote about the fact that thanksgiving helps us when we need to renew our strength because it slows us down and helps us to focus on the Lord and who He wants to be for us in the situation. It helps us to fill our gaze with the beauty of the Lord as we do that 'waiting'. A second reason why thanksgiving can help us to renew our strength is linked to the first because thanksgiving helps us to replace any negativity in our hearts and minds, with faith and hope.

Now we probably all know, but maybe don't fully realise, how draining negative thoughts can be. Just as we know that 'joy' gives strength, so we need to know that worrying, fretting, impatience, irritation etc., all drain energy from our 'system'. So does doubt, discouragement, disappointment and particularly emotions like resentment. You can give yourself a little check on this by asking yourself the question, "When do I feel most like springing out of bed in the morning?" i) When it's early but I have a flight booked to go on a great holiday that day, or ii) when it's normal waking time but there's a really hard day ahead of me, filled with things I'd rather not be doing, or iii) when I am carrying memories of my 'yesterday' that didn't go well?

Thanksgiving not only keeps my gaze on the Lord, who He is and what He has already done for me, it also helps me to process the negative draining thoughts and feelings. Thanksgiving fills us with hope, joy and an anticipation of His presence, rather than the kind of anticipation that makes us weary. This could be why, when we turn to the Lord to 'wait on Him' it needs to be totally different to when we pray about a situation. It can be so easy, if we just pray, to do our worrying on our knees and find that in fact we are using the time to rehearse our problems, (which the Lord knows about anyway!!)

'Waiting on the Lord', needs to be filled with praise and worship. It may well of course also involve telling the Lord our needs and requests, but we need to take the Apostle Paul's advice here as he encouraged the saints with these words, 'Devote yourselves to prayer, keeping alert in it with **an attitude of thanksgiving.**' (Colossians 4:2. NASB). The energy imparting thoughts and emotions, the natural antidotes to weariness, come as our mind is filled with positive things like hope, joy, vision, and faith. Thanksgiving helps to fill my mind with thoughts and memories of past 'triumphs' and interventions by the Lord, and hopes for future ones.

We can learn this from Jeremiah, who pours out his soul to the Lord in what sounds like desperation, and then says, 'Yet this I call to mind, and therefore I have hope:' (an energy inducing emotion) and so he continues, 'Because of the Lord's great love we are not consumed, for His compassions never fail. They are new every morning; great is your faithfulness. I say to myself, **"The Lord is my portion; therefore I will wait for Him."** (Lamentations 3:21-24).

This is wonderful 'self talk'. He is lifting his gaze to heaven and reminding himself of the Lord's love and mercy. He is also declaring his hope in the Lord's faithfulness for the future. So for us 'waiting on the Lord' to renew our strength when we are weary, will involve all those things too, and this can often begin with some simple thanksgiving.

Activation...

Next time you are feeling weary, spiritually, physically or emotionally, try some real waiting on the Lord. Choose to keep your focus on the Lord by having a heart of thanksgiving. Don't let your times of waiting be taken over with impatience and fretting, or even worry and fear.

That is to say, be like our dog when he is expecting some food. He doesn't move away from me, or take his eyes off of me until his bowl arrives full of good things to eat. Now that is what I see as hope filled expectant waiting!

DAY 193 | Thanksgiving and Mounting up on Eagles' Wings

Over the past couple of days we have been considering the promise from Isaiah 40:31, that those who 'wait upon the Lord shall renew their strength.' In that verse we are given the beautiful picture of the eagle mounting up on outstretched wings, in effortless flight, 'they will soar on wings like eagles'. I love seeing the footage of these magnificent birds on wildlife films. In this country we see the buzzards doing the same thing. They catch a thermal and can sometimes soar right out of sight to the naked eye, without even flapping a wing, it's that easy.

We have been talking about the fact that thanksgiving can help us to slow ourselves down and in this context the NASB translation, 'those who wait **for** the Lord', conveys something important for us. These amazing birds, eagles or buzzards, rise up as they spread their wings because they have waited **for** the thermal which will carry them upwards. They do rise up on their wings but that is because their wings act like sails and trap the power of the rising heat of the thermal underneath them. You can then see them circling around in an upward spiral. As the warm air rises they rise up too.

For us, if we liken ourselves to the eagle in this biblical metaphor, the thermal has got to be the Lord's love and presence with us. When we are weary and have no strength, it's time for us to spread our wings and catch the thermals of His love and His Spirit. Thanksgiving, as we said yesterday, will help us to focus on His goodness and will block those 'weary making' thoughts of discouragement and disappointment and now, in addition to that, we are talking about the 'lift' in our spirit that the Holy Spirit will give us as we turn to the Lord with gratitude in our hearts. This now becomes supernatural and we find ourselves 'soaring' in our spirit above all that would seek to drag us down.

One other piece of information about the eagle, which is relevant for us, is this. When the eagle soars it will apparently keep its eyes on the sun and, should the eagle espy or sense some turbulence ahead, it will rise higher and soar above and over the area of turbulence. The lesson for us I'm sure does not need spelling out. Our 'sun' is of course 'The Son', and keeping our eyes on Him will help us to rise in our spirits above those adverse circumstances that wear us down.

Thanksgiving enables us to 'wait **for**' the Lord, to catch the thermals of His love. It causes us, as we take a little time thinking and meditating on His goodness, to spread our wings in order to catch those thermals. Thanksgiving not only keeps our eyes on Him and our hearts open to Him, in faith and expectancy, but it also releases the Holy Spirit too. When the Holy Spirit sees our gratitude, He rushes in to do what He loves to do; to 'shed abroad the love of God in our hearts . . .' (Romans 5:5), in even greater measure.

So if we want to – 'run and not grow weary', and 'walk and not faint' – on our journey through life – 'thanksgiving' is a big key. It slows us down, causes us to 'gaze on Him' and draws the Holy Spirit, our alongside helper and strengthener to our aid faster than anything else, because He loves to be around us when we are grateful. We will find ourselves rising up as if on those eagle's wings, and also find our strength being renewed as we soar.

Activation ...

Today take some time to ponder on these wonderful words from a poem, 'Romanced by the Three.' by Jonathan Bugden. It's about our relationship with Father, Son and Holy Spirit and has been beautifully put to music by Dave Hadden on his album 'Heaven Sings' https://youtu.be/!TGOc2Juacc

> Peace, joy and wisdom reside in the three,
> But gladly and freely they're offered to me,
> That lifts me above the noise of my life
> Altering perception of struggle and strife,
> I can powerfully soar in the arms of the three.[1]

DAY 194 | Thanksgiving that Keeps us Alert

Over the last few days we have been reflecting on how thanksgiving can be a brilliant help to us as we wait on the Lord. We can find our strength being renewed even as we give thanks. It is important that this is not just theoretical, 'rising up on wings like an eagle' and 'running and not fainting', but it should be a very practical help to me when I am living in challenging or demanding times.

Sometimes 'weariness' can affect us when we are praying. Prayer, like Monday mornings, can be hard work when we are placing before the Lord people, situations, or battles, where a breakthrough is needed and we are longing to see those prayers answered. I was struck recently by Paul's words in Colossians 4:2-3, "Devote yourselves to prayer, keeping **alert**, with *an attitude of* thanksgiving, praying at the same time for us . . .". So let us now reflect on that little word 'alert'.

Now there are two sorts of **alertness**. One can be particularly prevalent today, where we see dishonesty, deception, lack of authenticity, and possible conspiracies all around us. There are scams, selling us a line, or a product, that isn't always what it says it is, and it can feel like people are always trying to get ahead of us, or get one over us. This is a reality in our fallen world, and so people can end up beyond healthy care and caution and find themselves in a place of general cynicism or at worst paranoia; '**alert**' for the next bad thing, or deception, coming their way.

We do need to be **alert** and aware and wise in our spiritual life too from our 'arch-scammer', the devil. Indeed Peter reminds us to, '. . . be on the **alert**. Your adversary, the devil, prowls around like a roaring lion, seeking someone to devour.' (1 Peter 5:8. NASB) The devil is a deceiver and the New Testament is clear that we need to be very **alert** not to be deceived by his, other people's, or even our own subtle deceptions. However we don't want to end up with a cynical attitude about everything. Jesus encouraged us to be wise (or shrewd) as serpents and harmless (or innocent) as doves. (Matthew 10:16).

Being alert spiritually in the more positive sense of being, awake and fresh, as in Paul's encouragement to stay alert in prayer, needs to include thanksgiving. Pressures, concerns, and worries can wear us down and make us flat even in prayer. 'Hope deferred makes the heart sick, but a longing fulfilled is a tree of life.' (Proverbs 13:12). But mix in plenty of thanksgiving, the air clears, **alertness** grows, and hope and faith return as we wait on the Lord. The Bible and the Lord are so practical – this is not just an encouragement to "Cheer up" but really practical guidance on how to catch the wind under your wings again – like the eagles.

I believe thanksgiving will help us to cultivate a healthy, positive, balanced **alertness**. We need to be people who know that there is a good deal of deception in the natural and spiritual world around us, but who are also very **alert** to the grace, promises and power of the Lord. So back to Colossians 4:2, let us stay **alert** in our times of pressures, and the challenges that cause us to call on God in prayer, by seasoning these times with a very healthy dose of thanksgiving. This will surely clear our minds and emotions, and help us 'see the wood for the trees' from God's perspective. It will enable us to be **alert** to His wonderful love, goodness and power.

As I give thanks I will see that the problem that I am praying about is also an opportunity for me to see God at work; keeping His promises and showing His incredible grace, power and love to and for me. It will renew clarity and **alertness**. By God's grace my eyes will be opened, as were Elisha's servant's eyes and I may 'see' that, "Those who are with us are more than those who are with them." (2 Kings 6:16,17) The **alertness** and the light that thanksgiving engenders will lift my spirits and inject fresh hope and faith, and will then probably lead on to even more thanksgiving.

Activation...

When you pray today, pray 'with thanksgiving' and see what a difference it makes to your faith and persistence in asking. See how it alters your perception of the situation and releases God's wisdom to you in sometimes quite unexpected ways.

DAY 195 | Thanksgiving that Draws the Holy Spirit Close

I wrote recently that the Holy Spirit loves gratitude and thanksgiving, and that when he sees our gratitude, He rushes in to do what He loves to do, to 'shed abroad the love of God in our hearts...' (Romans 5:5), in even greater measure. That set me thinking about the Holy Spirit, and about what He loves and what grieves Him.

We read in Ephesians that what comes out of our mouths is very important in this respect. 'Do not let any unwholesome talk come out of your mouths, but only what is helpful for building others up according to their needs, that it might benefit those who listen. **And do not grieve the Holy Spirit of God**, with whom you are sealed for the day of redemption. Get rid of all bitterness, rage and anger, brawling and slander, along with every form of malice. Be kind and compassionate to one another, forgiving each other, just as in Christ God forgave you.' (Ephesians 4:29-32).

Wow, quite a list. Was he really writing to Christians we wonder? Well yes! and he was probably thinking about what Jesus said about our mouths letting everyone know what is in our hearts. "For out of the overflow of the heart the mouth speaks." (Matthew 12:34). What we entertain in our hearts and partner with in our thoughts, will eventually burst out of our mouths unless we allow the Holy Spirit to help us. He knows what is in our hearts before it comes out, and He knows what is in our hearts even if we hold it all in and let nothing out!!

We know that we are sealed with the Holy Spirit, so when we 'grieve Him' it is not about Him leaving us. He will find a way to let us know when we have grieved Him; He will be specific about what it is and He will be there to help us, but if we ignore His prompting He may well go very quiet on us. If we look next at what happened to Jesus when He visited Nazareth for example, we will find a second category of thoughts and words that grieve the Spirit, causing Him to 'go quiet'.

We read that 'He could not do any miracles there, except lay His hands on a few sick people and heal them.' Now we know that Jesus was no less anointed by the Holy Spirit than at any other time during His three year ministry on earth, and so we read that Jesus was, 'amazed at their lack of faith.' (Mark 6:5,6). Jesus had done the most amazing things all around the country after leaving the wilderness, 'in the power of the Spirit' (Luke 4:14), but not here in Nazareth. The Holy Spirit, it would appear, had gone very quiet.

The people in Nazareth had somehow been offended by Jesus' teaching and wisdom, and were saying something like, "Who does He think He is?" As far as they were concerned He was just a carpenter with whom they had grown up. (Mark 6:3). So there were no signs and wonders in Nazareth and we don't read of Jesus ever returning there again. Out of the mouths of the people in Nazareth came doubt, unbelief, skepticism, judgment and ultimately the rejection of Jesus. Clearly the Holy Spirit was grieved.

A third way in which we can grieve the Holy Spirit is spelt out to us by Paul in his letter to the Thessalonians. He encourages them to, 'Be joyful always; pray continually; give thanks in all circumstances, for this is God's will for you in Christ Jesus. **Do not put out the Spirit's fire; do not treat prophecies with contempt. Test everything. Hold onto the good. Avoid every kind of evil.**' (1 Thessalonians 5:16-22).

From these scriptures, we can see that there are three specific things that 'grieve' the Holy Spirit; things to avoid if we are to honour and draw Him fully into our lives. They are:-

i) Anger, malice and lack of forgiveness.

ii) Unbelief, criticism, cynicism, and judgement.

iii) Contempt for spiritual gifting and utterance.

If it is those negative thoughts and feelings in our hearts and on our lips that grieve the Holy Spirit, then it is more important than ever that we fill our hearts with gratitude and speak out thanksgiving. As we do, we will be filling ourselves up with the opposite of those attitudes that quench or grieve Him.

Activation . . .

Today guard your heart from all these attitudes by filling your heart with gratitude; then what comes out of your mouth from your heart will be pleasing to the Holy Spirit, good for your hearers, and good for you too.

DAY 196 | Opening the Sluice Gates!

Today we are going to think some more about how we can allow the Holy Spirit to flow freely through our lives, and the picture I have in my mind is of the sluice gates that control the flow of water in and out of a canal lock gate. So, if you can, imagine that you are in a canal boat going up in a lock. You will find yourself in quite a tight place. There are brick walls to left and right, and big wooden gates to the front and the back.

The 'paddles' are the openings in the gates. They are like windows, often below the surface of the water and, unless you open them in the gate in front of you, no water will enter your lock and you will not rise up to the level of the higher water on the other side of the lock gate. Because of the weight of water behind the gates, you do not have the strength to push the gates open, even a fraction, in order to let that water in. Basically you will not be going anywhere anytime soon. It would appear that you are stuck!

The situation will, however, totally change if those paddles are opened, even if just a little, because then the water will flow into the lock. The boat, and everything and everyone in it, will rise up quite quickly and effortlessly until the water is level with the water on the other side of the lock gate. Then the lock gates will open and you can move forwards on the canal.

The parallels here are numerous, so let us imagine we are the boat, (or are in the boat). The water represents the Holy Spirit carrying us along the path of life, and the lock represents a challenge that comes our way in life; a difficult situation, a relationship, or a decision that needs to be made. The situation can seem like the lock – a bit of a tight place and we are stuck. How are we are going to move past this place in which we find ourselves?

In yesterday's meditation we were looking at those things that grieve the Holy Spirit. Things like unbelief, criticism, gossip, unforgiveness, in fact anything that is negative towards ourselves, towards others, or even God Himself. Things that, in this picture of the lock, keep Him locked out of our situation, and unable to flow freely into our lives to bring His wisdom, grace and strength. These things prevent us from being lifted up and carried forward by the Holy Spirit. So what can we do to open those paddles again? What will enable the Holy Spirit to flow freely into our lives? Yes!! Yet again it can be that simple act of 'Giving Thanks'!

The parallels continue here, because anyone who has ever tried to open the paddles with a lock key will know that they are very stiff to start with, and sometimes giving thanks can feel a bit like hard work until we get going. We may even have to start by thanking Him for, our home, bread to eat, the air we breathe etc. Then we can move on to thanking Him that He is with us in our difficulty, and that He has the wisdom that we need. But always remember that those paddles only have to open just a little bit to let the water flow into the lock in order to start raising the boat.

Moving through a lock, as you can imagine, is not a rushed job. It is not like leaving the traffic lights, revving the car and going from 0 to 60 in a few seconds. Obviously the wider we open the paddles the faster the water flows into the lock and the faster the boat will rise up in the water, so being radical with our thanksgiving 'pays off' in the long run. Even letting the water rise up quickly however, does still need patience. So as we turn our hearts to thanksgiving in a situation, we will need patience and persistence before we can leave that lock.

The final parallel is this. Having raised the boat to the next level of water in order to be able to move on, we will see the landscape which was out of sight whilst we were in the lock. And so through giving thanks we will also have gained a new perspective on our situation, and perhaps that is the most important thing of all. Thanksgiving will enable us to rise up to see our situation and other people the way God sees them.

Activation...

If there is a situation in your life that feels 'stuck' determine today to give thanks for as many things as you can. Determine to thank Him until you sense the Holy Spirit with all His love and wisdom flowing into your heart and mind with all His creative solutions to the issue. Canal boating can be hard work but fun. In this way let your journey through life with the Holy Spirit also become challenging but fun. Enjoy!!

DAY 197 | Thanksgiving that Brings Jesus Joy

Have you ever tried to give someone a compliment, only to find that it has been deflected away. This could be an attempt at false modesty, a genuine mistrust of 'unnecessary' flattery, or it could even be a fear of becoming conceited or proud. You will hear things like, "Oh really? Well it was nothing much", or "Thank you but I do need to...", or "but it wasn't as good as..." or even the spiritual one, "It was the Lord, not me".

The feeling you get when you get that kind of response is quite different to the joy that you feel when your compliment (providing it is genuine) has been gladly received, and the person receiving it has 'glowed' with their own joy of being appreciated, or affirmed.

I sometimes think that I can be rather like that with God. I used to feel when I heard a word of encouragement, a prophecy or a scripture, telling me how much the Lord loves me, or that I bring Him joy, that He was really just saying nice things because He has to, or because He wanted to make me feel better. After all, it says in the bible that God, 'so loved the world...,' (John 3:16), so my thinking was that I am just included in that general feeling of benevolence which God has towards His creation. **It somehow wasn't personal.**

I wasn't aware that I was not fully receiving God's love for me, nor how that could be grieving the Lord, until in one meeting, as we were singing that beautiful chorus 'I love you Lord, and I lift my voice, to worship you, Oh my soul rejoice'. I felt that the Holy Spirit was encouraging me to change the words and sing '**You** love **me** Lord, and I lift my voice to worship you...'. Well, it just felt wrong, proud, perhaps a bit deluded. The thoughts going through my head were, "It couldn't be God asking me to change the words like that, and would that still be worship? I think not!"

It reminds me of the Shulammite Bride in the Song of Songs. When she is told she is the 'most beautiful among women' (Song of Songs 1:8), she feels that because she has been out in the fields looking after the sheep, and has been darkened by the sun, that she is not very beautiful, and so she tells them not to look at her, (Verse 6). Not a good example of how to receive a compliment, and if we take the spiritual interpretation and consider that she represents the 'Bride of Christ' – us!!! We could do well to learn from her mistakes.

In this meeting to which I was referring however, the Holy Spirit seemed to be insistent, and so I tried it out!!! I changed the words around – and it was OK. In fact it was more than OK, it was as if my declaration that the Lord loved me not only released faith into my heart – that He really did, but it also felt like I was actually giving the Lord joy because I was believing Him and worshipping Him for the wonder of that truth. **It became personal.** He didn't just love 'the world', He truly loved 'ME'! When someone receives my compliment, or my expression of affection or appreciation, it draws us closer and seals our friendship. So in a similar way acknowledging, receiving and delighting in the fact that I am loved by God, draws me closer to Him and enriches our friendship in an unfathomable way.

It says in Zephaniah 3:17, 'The Lord your God is in the midst of you ... He will rejoice over you with joy, He will rest [in silent satisfaction] and in His love He will be silent and make no mention (of past sins ...); He will exalt over you with singing.' (AMP). It almost seems from this translation, as if God can rest in His joy over us when He knows that 'we've got it'; when we have received and are enjoying the reality of His love for us. I still find it staggering that I bring Jesus 'joy', but we were created for His joy, and 'it was for the joy set before Him' – that is you and me becoming His – that He went to the cross. (Hebrews 12:2).

Activation ...

Today let your thanksgiving give God great joy. Let Him hear you speak out or sing of your gratitude and joy at being loved individually and personally by Him.

He has paid a great price to show that love to you; receive it in a very personal way as you express your grateful thanks to Him. You may be surprised by how close to Him you will begin to feel, as the truth of His great, personal and all embracing love seeps ever deeper into your heart.

DAY 198 | Thanksgiving for our 'Garments of Splendour'

Today let's think a little more about the Shulammite Bride, in the Song of Songs. She couldn't accept that she was, to her lover, 'the most beautiful of women' (Song of Songs 1:8), because she had been out working in the fields. She may have felt sunburnt, and also a bit scruffy and very 'unglamorous'. She wasn't, at that point, dressed in her bridle attire, and I am wondering if that is why some of us find it hard to believe that the Lord rejoices and sings over us, (Zephaniah 3:17). Could it be that we haven't yet fully grasped that we are clothed in a beauty that earth cannot comprehend?

If you are seeking to follow the Lord, you will be aware that you are being, 'transformed into His likeness with ever increasing glory, which **comes from the Lord, who is the Spirit.**' (2 Corinthians 3:18). You will also be aware of the failures that still seem to 'hang around you', and our enemy will surely keep you conscious of those things on a daily basis. His weapon in this area is discouragement as he whispers to us, pointing out our shortcomings.

Like the Shulammite, we can feel, 'I've been working very hard, but I feel rather dirty and scruffy right now spiritually speaking.' If so, it is time that we listened to our heavenly bridegroom and put on our 'robes of righteousness'. We need to join Isaiah in his song to the Lord, 'I delight greatly in the Lord; my soul rejoices in my God. For He has clothed me with garments of salvation and arrayed me in a robe of righteousness, as a bridegroom adorns his head like a priest, and as a bride adorns herself with her jewels. For as the soil makes the sprout come up and a garden causes seed to grow, so the Sovereign Lord will make righteousness and praise spring up before all the nations.' (Isaiah 61:10,11).

Isaiah was speaking long before Jesus died for us on the cross, and yet he knew that God's people were to be a demonstration to the world of the Lord's righteousness and praise. They were going to be spiritually 'stunning'. How much more should we, who are part of the divine exchange – His righteousness for my sinfulness – celebrate that we are now clothed in His righteousness before the throne of God, and that we are therefore very beautiful in the eyes of the whole of heaven. Jesus wants us, His waiting bride, to know that we are clothed in garments of splendour.

'For if by the trespass of one man, death reigned through that one man, how much more will those who receive God's abundant provision of grace and of the gift of righteousness reign in life through the one man, Jesus Christ.' (Romans 5:17). The plan is that we wear that robe of righteousness by faith, so that we can reign in life and be a demonstration to the world of the goodness of God. It is not to His glory that we go around feeling 'grubby'!!

In the parable of the prodigal son, (which is actually more about the Father's heart), Jesus spells out the Father's intention for us. After the boy had come back to a wonderful reunion and restoration he had 'the best robe' put around his shoulders. (Luke 15:22). I find that incredibly moving. No more dirty pig sty clothes for this lad. In that simple act his dignity, status and sonship was totally restored. Being clothed in His righteousness, even when I still keep making mistakes and messing up, is part of the 'outrageous grace of God' that the elder brother in the story couldn't cope with.

Hundreds of years ago God spoke to an apostate nation, calling them back to Himself, "Awake, awake. O Zion, clothe yourself with strength. Put on your garments of splendor, O Jerusalem ... Shake off your dust; rise up, sit enthroned, O Jerusalem ..." (Isaiah 52:1,2). Today, let us fill our hearts with thanksgiving for the beautiful robes that the Lord has given us and wear them boldly. As Jarrod Cooper wrote 25 years ago in his beautiful song, 'King of Kings' – 'In Royal robes, I don't deserve, I live to serve your majesty'.

Activation ...

Think how differently you enter a room when you are feeling well dressed and smart. It alters your whole demeanor.

Today wear your garments of splendour with thanksgiving. As you express your gratitude, it will alter how you walk through the day.

Give thanks that because of Jesus you are clothed in beauty and splendour, and see the difference that it makes to how you think, speak and behave.

DAY 199 | Thanksgiving for all the 'Good Things' in Others

Sometimes in our thanksgiving journey, we just have to circle back to some very basic truths, like the fact that to be grateful, and to be able to express that gratitude, is a very profound gift that God has given humankind. It is a huge antidote to the potential that we have to easily, and quite naturally, see flaws and mistakes, glitches and problems.

In some respects seeing those flaws and problems is good, because it helps us to stay safe in difficult situations and improve things in others. For some people this is part of their job. We want our doctor to see what is wrong with us and we want the safety officer to detect problems before an accident happens, but if we wear those glasses that critique everything all the time, especially in the church, or among our friends and family, we become uncomfortable people to be around and our focus on what is wrong, or on what can be improved can cause distance and separation.

Yesterday we were thinking about how the Lord rejoices over us, not because we suddenly became perfect when we became Christians, but because He sees us through the eyes of a Saviour. He sees us in our beautiful garments of splendor, the robes of righteousness for which He paid such a huge price. He still plans to change us to become like Himself, but He celebrates the choice we made to accept that offer of forgiveness and to lay our lives before Him, so that we are today clothed in, and live for, His glory.

It is important that we recognise that Jesus sees us in this way, so that we can in turn view others through His eyes. I wonder if this was part of Paul's thinking when he wrote, 'So from now on we regard no one from a worldly point of view. Though we once regarded Christ in this way, we do so no longer. Therefore, if anyone is in Christ, he is a new creation; the old has gone, the new has come!' (2 Corinthians 5:16,17). Paul realises that he nearly missed the Messiah because he was viewing him through the wrong lens, and so he was looking for and finding fault with His teaching and claims. The Authorised Version translates this phrase as, 'we recognise no man after the flesh:' which I think is helpful in this context.

If we view our brothers and sisters, 'after the flesh', we may well find that we miss some very precious things that the Lord has done and is doing in their lives. If we only find ourselves looking at their shortcomings and faults, instead of seeing them with the same lens of faith and kindness with which Christ views us, we will not be able to encourage and envision them for the purposes that God has for them. Just remember that the nation of Israel was in quite a mess when the Lord spoke to them declaring, 'You will be a crown of splendor in the Lord's hand, a royal diadem in the hand of your God.' (Isaiah 62:3).

In Jesus' last prayer for His followers He says, "I pray also for those who will believe in me through their message, that all of them may be one, Father, just as you are in me and I am in you. May they also be in us so that the world may believe that you sent me. **I have given them the glory that you gave me, that they may be one as we are one**: I in them and you in me. May they be brought to complete unity to let the world know that you sent me and have loved them even as you have loved me." (John 17:20-23).

The interesting thing here is that none of the disciples were perfect from that point on after this prayer. Some like Peter made big mistakes. This wasn't about suddenly becoming perfect, but about being united as carriers of the glory of God. Jesus Himself had given them His glory, and He wanted their unity to be about the fact that He was living in each one of them.

If I can stay with a heart of thankfulness for my brothers and sisters, thanking God that He lives in them and that He is at work in each precious life for His glory, then I will be able to bless them more freely. I will also be able to rejoice in their victories, and point them to the grace of God that they are needing in order to walk as Jesus would have them walk.

Activation ...

Make sure today that you are viewing your brothers and sisters through the right lens by first and foremost giving thanks for them, so that you are seeing them 'not after the flesh' but as a 'new creation'. One that is being beautifully moulded and transformed into His likeness.

DAY 200 | Thanksgiving and Following Jesus!

There is much talk today about 'followers', and about how many 'followers' people have, and of course we are talking here about 'followers' on the internet, on Twitter or Instagram. People put up their posts and those who are interested in what they have to say will get a notification and will be able to read the latest thoughts or exploits of the one who they are 'following'. They may of course end up copying this person, or believing something that they have written, but they may never meet the person and will be able to pick and choose from the comfort of their own home, what particular 'posts' they want to take notice of, or copy.

When Jesus said, 'Come, follow me', (Mark 1:16 and Mark 2:14), He was not talking about "have a listen and see if you like my ideas", He was calling those people to leave everything to go with Him; to see and be a part of everything He was going to be doing. He was calling them to be His disciples, those who would give their lives to Him, to be led and taught by Him and, after His Ascension and Pentecost, to be indwelt by Him. This was something intensely personal and commanding. It was an 'all in', or 'all out', experience for them and they definitely wanted to be 'all in'.

I love that Jesus said, 'Follow Me'. How different from the slave driver who drives from behind with a whip or a stick. When Jesus calls us to follow Him He has always gone ahead and draws us from the front. We follow but He leads, He shows us the way as we stay near. When Jesus says 'Follow Me' His intention is that we will have a close and ongoing relationship. He speaks of Himself as the 'Good Shepherd', who leads and guards His sheep in such a personal relationship that He was able to say of those sheep, 'they will hear my voice;' (John 10:16, NASB). Now that is close and intimate.

Another beautiful thing about 'following Jesus' is that Jesus **leads** us. He doesn't call us to follow Him, as it were, through a jungle or a swamp. He doesn't forge ahead leaving us fighting through undergrowth, struggling to keep up, and afraid that we are about to lose sight of Him. Nor does He allow us to drop out because we are so far behind but He didn't notice. His leading is more like a dance partner who says "follow my lead", and I will guide you through the steps, and I will set the direction and speed. The lovely thing about this kind of leading and following, is that it means that He wants to keep in very close contact with us, so that we can hear His whispers as He guides us across the dance floor of life.

Finally we need to know that Jesus doesn't lead us at a pace we cannot sustain. Nor does He lead us like a mountain Sherpa who has forgotten to make sure we are equipped with the right gear. He is 'the Lord my Shepherd' and I know that He will make sure that I lack nothing for the journey we are on. He will lead me by still waters when I need them, and into green pastures when my soul needs restoring. He will also lead me in the right paths. I can trust His leading and I can follow without fear of going the wrong way. (Psalm 23:1-3).

Sometimes however we can feel like we've got disconnected from our Heavenly Leader. We can find it hard to follow because we are not entirely sure which way He has gone. We know He is ahead somewhere but we've got distracted along the way and are not entirely sure which way to go. This could be from one extreme to another. We can feel lost, for example, over a major decision in life, or just lost in the course of a day; so what do we do then?

I believe thanksgiving is the biggest connector ever. Just thanking Jesus that He is there for me, just ahead, brings Him back into view. Thanking Him that He is equipping me for this part of the journey releases my faith to expect, and receive, the grace that I am needing to follow Him. And lastly, but perhaps most importantly, thanking Him that 'His goodness and love will follow me all the days of my life', (Psalm 23:6), and that includes today. Thanking Him will draw me back into His arms of love, back into the dance and allow me to 'follow Him' with joy in my heart again.

Activation...

Simply give thanks today, throughout the day, that He is your Good Shepherd, friend and guide. Your thanksgiving is a wonderful expression of faith that He is very close and leading you through the day. Then I believe you will be able to see and hear Him more clearly, and rejoice in His presence moment by moment.

DAY 201 | Thanksgiving and the Call of Jesus

I was a relatively young Christian at a Christian convention, and I was being offered a place at a Bible College if I would just sign up there and then. It felt like it could be a 'Follow Me' moment. Was Jesus asking me to leave everything, i.e my University course, to follow Him? This would be very costly in terms of telling my non Christian parents, but was this part of me 'taking up my cross' to 'follow Him'? (Matthew 10:38). I was confused and a bit scared: Scared of disobeying the Lord and missing an 'open door' opportunity in front of me and my moment to demonstrate my commitment and faith to the Lord, but also sacred of 'stepping out in faith' and risking everything by making a big mistake.

Well, new Christian as I was, I had already had some good teaching and had learnt a few scriptures. I knew somehow that it wasn't the Lord's way to hustle us into things, and so the pressure to make an immediate decision put on a warning light for me, even though I knew that the disciples left their boats and **immediately** followed Jesus when He called them. Years later, I did realise that, in fact, the disciples had probably already been watching Jesus, and may well have already had that hunger stirring in their hearts to get close to Him, before He called them. (Mark 1:16-20).

Back to my journey with the offer of a place at Bible College; so, feeling very churned up, I decided to take a step back and think a little more about this decision. That is when the Holy Spirit 'dropped' into my mind the scripture from John 10:3-5 about the sheep 'knowing the voice' of the one who is leading them, 'the sheep listen to His voice. He calls his own sheep by name and **leads** them out ... he **goes on ahead of them**, and his sheep **follow** him because they know his voice. But they will never follow a stranger ...'

It was a good moment. Peace was restored, and I knew that this wasn't Jesus' way of **leading,** because I was feeling **'driven'**. That fearful condemning voice challenging me to prove myself and my faith was not God. So there it is; the wonderful truth that we are called to **'follow'** Jesus, as He goes ahead and **leads** us. His voice is a beckoning, "Let's, Me and you, have an adventure" kind of voice, not a "Do this or you're a failure!" voice. I suspect that when Jesus called those first disciples to follow Him, they heard that beckoning in His voice and saw it on His face too.

One time when the disciples were in a tight spot, trying to get across Lake Galilee on a very windy night, they see what they think is a ghost walking across to them on the water. Jesus calls to them "Take courage! It is I. Don't be afraid." Peter then responds with the famous statement, "Lord, if it is you, tell me to come to you." I love it that Jesus just said, "Come". No persuasion, or reassurance "It's really me!", or long explanation about how to walk on water; He just said "Come". What was it in that word 'Come' that gave Peter the faith to do the impossible and get out of the boat? (Matthew 14:22-32).

I think it was that Peter knew his Master's voice. He had heard Jesus say that word 'Come' many times in many different ways and contexts, to many different people. Something in that voice put the faith in his heart that enabled him to do what no one else has ever done. Jesus beckoned him and he followed. Let us learn from this that Jesus' voice doesn't 'goad' it 'guides'.

We probably all know that there are many other checks that will help us in discerning the Lord's voice. Clearly whatever the real Jesus asks us to do will never contravene what is written down for us in the Bible. We can also seek wise counsel from friends, family and pastors. Then there is the 'peace' that the Holy Spirit brings when we 'follow' His promptings and leadings. Paul's advice is to 'let the peace of Christ rule in your hearts . . . **And be thankful.***'* (Colossians 3:15).

Activation ...

So if you are ever in a bit of turmoil – not knowing if the Lord is leading you in a situation, big or small – turn to Him with thanksgiving in your heart that He is your 'Good Shepherd'. At those times you can say to Him, *"I want to thank you Lord that I can and do hear you voice, and I thank you that it is recognisable because your voice beckons, releasing grace to me, and it gives me peace. Amen.*

Giving thanks will help you to tune in to His voice. You will hear His 'Come', even if it does feel like He is asking you to walk on the water. His voice doesn't drive, or use guilt and fear. He leads by inviting and beckoning; and you'll sense the joy in His heart as you follow His leading.

DAY 202 | The Prism that is Thanksgiving

After I had my cataracts removed a while ago, I could undoubtedly see things very much more clearly and in richer colour than I had become used to but, mysteriously, I still found that if, for example, I looked at the moon I would see two moons, a bright moon and a shadow moon overlaying it. A recent visit to the optician proved to be very helpful in that I was given an explanation of the cause of, and solution to, this phenomenon.

I had astigmatism. Astigmatism distorts what we are seeing. It skews it. It's a structural defect that prevents the rays of light from both eyes being brought to a common focus and so the image is not sharp. So, although my distance eyesight was very good, I was told that putting a prism into my new lens would correct this defect.

I thought this morning, "that is what our culture does to our view of God", and "that is what the atmospheres all around us do over time. They behave like an astigmatism, distorting our vision of who God is, and His amazingly beautiful characteristics."

I fell to thinking about the prism that the optician has prescribed for me, in order that I should see the moon and other distant objects more clearly, and it seemed like the Lord was saying that 'the prism of thanksgiving' is the thing that will clear the distortions from our vision of Him. The 'prism of thanksgiving' will enable us to filter out all the distortions that the world puts on our God, and we will be able to see Him clearly in all His magnificence.

Then, as I was ruminating on this, a further wonderful thought crossed my mind. Thinking of prisms I went back in time to my science class, when we played with prisms and white light, and saw for ourselves the incredible constituents of white light spread before us in the full spectrum of the rainbow. Just amazing! As you know, we have never lost our fascination with those rainbow colours, and I believe this is what the Lord said to me in that moment.

"If My people will look at me through the prism of thanksgiving, not only will they see more clearly who I AM, they will see My Power and My Love for them brighter, stronger and clearer every day. They will also begin to see My Glory as on the Mount Of Transfiguration shining in all its splendor and colour into their lives. My desire is to have a people who, like Moses, will say to Me, "Show me your Glory", and who will then see My Goodness and Loving Kindness pass before their eyes." (See Exodus 33:18-19, 34:6,7).

We need to have our gaze on our wonderful God, freed from the cynicism, rationalism and humanism of our day. A heart of thanksgiving will ensure that not only will we see Him more clearly and sharply, but we will also see the magnificent kaleidoscope of colour that is our God; the fullness of His power, His love, and His goodness. Then we will be able to authentically reflect who He is to our sad and cynical world.

Activation ...

Today use the prism of thanksgiving to correct your view of God. Let the Holy Spirit help you to see where your vision has become distorted and give thanks for the truths that He highlights to you from the scriptures.

You could even write down here any 'distortions' that you become aware of and then the truths that you now 'see' that replace those distortions.

Then pray ...

Lord I ask that you will give me 20/20 spiritual vision with no astigmatism, that I may see you in all your glory, and reflect your colourful beauty to those around me at this time. Amen.

DAY 203 | Thanksgiving for the 'Exchange'

When Jesus stood in the synagogue in Nazareth and quoted the amazing prophecy written down for us in Isaiah 61:1-3,6, He confirmed that it was indeed His Messianic mission statement. The prophecy tells us that the Spirit of the Lord would be on the Messiah, anointing Him to 'preach good news to the poor, bind up the broken hearted, proclaim freedom to the captives and release for the prisoners'. He is also going to 'proclaim the year of the Lord's favour and the day of vengeance of our God'. It then goes directly on to state that the Messiah is going to 'comfort all who mourn,' in three different ways.

Firstly they are to be given 'beauty for ashes'. The Messiah is going to give the grieving ones something beautiful to put on their heads **instead of** the ashes which would have marked them out as being in mourning. Secondly they were going to be given, 'the oil of gladness **instead of** mourning'. This was an anointing fragrance not associated with someone in grief, and thirdly they were to be given 'the garment of praise **instead of** a spirit of despair': Again the point being that people in mourning don't usually dress in 'happy' clothes. (Bold emphasis is mine)

The provision for those who grieve is threefold, giving it great emphasis. All three pictures, taken from normal grieving practice, denote the exchange that the Messiah will bring spiritually, emotionally and physically to His people. The description of this exchange follows on from the fact that the Messiah is proclaiming the year of the Lord's favour and the day of vengeance of our God. God is going to pour His favour on His people **and avenge them for the damage that the enemy has done to them,** that left them in mourning.

The parallels for us are immense. I believe that an important part of our Salvation, beyond our new birth, is seeing the damage that the enemy has done in our lives reversed. Many of us are comforted by these promises but we don't always find that we are fully able to enter in to all that they offer; our delight in these promises is not always matched by our ability to appropriate them. I was struck this morning by the fact that the Authorised Version uses the word 'for' where the other versions use 'instead of', and I think that this holds a clue for us by conveying something very important as we look to benefit from these promises and receive these gifts from our Saviour.

When I give you something 'for' something else, there is an exchange. Think about it. In a game of Monopoly, if I give you my four railway stations 'for' Mayfair and Park Lane, I no longer own the Railway stations, but I do own Mayfair and Park Lane. When I get something 'for' something else, it means there is something I have to 'give' or let go of first, in order to receive the desired thing.

Sometimes we want to hold onto our stuff **and** take what Jesus offers, but it doesn't work like that. Taking the 'stuff' that makes us grieve in any way, shape, or form to the cross, and leaving it there, is a necessary first step to receiving the benefits of living in 'the year of the Lord's favour'. So how can I know that I have left my 'heaviness' at the cross? Well one way is to thank Jesus for 'taking' my sorrows and my grief, (Isaiah 53:4), and that may cover many different things, then I thank Him for what He is giving me in exchange. Two lots of 'Thank You' are needed!!!

In case this should all seem too good to be true, let's look at the rest of these verses. Isaiah prophesies that these people who have experienced this divine exchange will go on to rebuild things, renew cities, have flocks and vineyards, and be called priests of the Most High. (Isaiah 61:4-6). God clearly has plans for them. These people who have experienced this divine exchange are to be part of His restoration team for the nation. God wants this divine exchange to happen because He loves us? Yes! And also for His Kingdom's sake.

Activation ...

So today if there are some things for which you need a divine exchange, name and take them to the cross with thanksgiving in your heart. Let Him take them from you, knowing that He wants them and has paid a price for them. Then thank Him as you receive all that He is longing to give you in exchange. Write those things down and keep giving thanks for them as you go on receiving in the days ahead.

DAY 204 | Thanksgiving and Peace

When we find ourselves in a difficult situation, or concerned about someone we love, I guess it's an automatic reaction to 'pray', to talk to God. Whether it's a short sharp 'HELP' kind of prayer, a long deep intercessory prayer, or anything in between, we are often motivated by the circumstances that we see before us. Quite often, if we are honest, our praying is driven by our worries and concerns. Our prayers are fuelled by our need for God's help and intervention in the situation because we don't have the answers, or the ability in ourselves to change things for the better. How often do we hear people say, "Well, all we can do is pray." No wonder therefore that prayer is often linked to those times of 'feeling anxious'.

Paul, in his letter to the Philippian church, gets that. He writes to them, 'Do not be anxious about anything, but in everything, by prayer and petition, with thanksgiving, present your requests to God. And the peace of God, which transcends all understanding, will guard your hearts, and your minds in Christ Jesus.' (Philippians 4:6,7). Paul knows, probably from firsthand experience, that being anxious and prayer often go together, and they can often stay together as, in our minds, we turn the problem over as we pray. If we are not careful we are actually meditating on the issues, filling our minds with them, hoping that God is listening in as we chew it all over.

At some point we might hit upon the answer so that we can tell God what we would like Him to do, or offer Him some advice on the best way to tackle it. Unfortunately, we often can't see or don't have the faith for what needs to happen, and so our rumination feeds our fears and our prayer becomes the proverbial 'worrying on our knees'.

I love the phrase that Paul uses here, 'with thanksgiving present your requests to God', or literally in the Greek 'with thanksgivings the requests of you let be made known to God.' The implication is clear. I don't have to help God to come up with an answer. I don't even have to help Him by explaining in detail how bad it all is. I can just 'present my requests to Him', and if I don't even know what to 'request' I can pray in tongues, or I can just say, "Lord my request is that your Kingdom comes in this situation for your glory." That's a prayer that will always be answered. So why does Paul encourage us to make our requests **'with thanksgiving'**? I think for two main reasons.

Firstly it expresses my trusting relationship with Him, my Good, Good, Father. It expresses that I'm confident that He is hearing me, cares about me, and is constantly working on my behalf, for my good and His glory. It helps me to know that I don't need to persuade Him to be involved. Maybe this illustration helps. When I give a waiter or waitress my food order, I usually say "thank you" with a smile, because I know that they have heard what I want, have noted it down and that they will be bringing it to me in due course. Thanking God as I 'present my requests' says to Him, "I love you Father and I know you love me, and that you have heard my request; I am now trusting you for your answer."

The second reason for 'presenting our request **with thanksgiving**, is for our 'peace of mind and heart'. We may well have been led by the Spirit as we 'presented our request to God', but what about our wayward heart and mind **after** we have finished praying. 'Faith' can be expressed in the moment of prayer, but what happens in the next twenty four hours in our hearts and minds is vitally important if we are to stay in faith.

Thanksgiving can help to prevent our thoughts, or our feelings, from slipping back into anxiety. Paul says that the peace of God, which transcends all understanding will 'stand guard' over our thoughts and feelings. Thanking God that He has got my request in His heart, **every time that issue comes back to mind**, enables God's peace to flow into my heart and mind, preventing or rebuffing the invasion of any doubts and unbelief.

Activation...

What a wonderful gift thanksgiving is!! Determine today that from now on you will always weave thanksgiving into all your times of prayer, however long or short they may be.

DAY 205 | Thanksgiving for Abundant Supplies of Grace

I wonder how you woke up this morning? Fresh as the proverbial daisy? Feeling overwhelmed by what today holds? Feeling tired from a night of tossing and turning? Or excited by all the possibilities today brings? Probably for most of us there is a bit of a kaleidoscope going on in our thoughts with all of those things running through our minds in turn. It may well be that not many of us wake up every day singing 'This is the day that the Lord hath made; we will rejoice and be glad in it.' (Psalm 118:24. AV).

Well this morning I was reminded again that whatever the day brings and however I slept and awoke, there will never be a shortage of grace for everything that the day holds. Now that **is** something to be thankful for!! Grace sufficient for every eventuality is always available, and because grace is itself given to us 'through' grace, the supply of grace will never be dependent on, or as a result of, my performance. Now that is something else to be very thankful about!!

Grace will be available to keep us overcoming in all circumstances, at the same time as keeping us totally humble, because we can say with Paul, 'Not that we are sufficient of ourselves to think anything as of ourselves; but our sufficiency is of God.' (2 Corinthians 3:5. AV). It is also in that same letter that Paul reminds the Corinthians that 'God is able to make all grace abound to you, so that in all things at all times, **having all you need**, you will abound to every good work.' (2 Corinthians 9:8).

Having 'sufficient' grace in every situation, can feel like, "Phew, I just made it through!" It can feel like getting to the end of the month with relief that there were 'sufficient' funds for all the standing orders and the shopping bills. 'Sufficient' can feel like 'enough but no extra', but the difference between the bank of heaven and my high street, or online bank is that the heavenly bank has a never ending supply of grace pouring into our account, and the more we need to take out the more grace that pours in. In the language of heaven, 'sufficient' means 'way more than enough' for each situation.

The fact is I can never be in a situation where the 'grace' account has gone into overdraft. I will never get that letter that says, 'You have exceeded your agreed overdraft so charges will now be incurred, and no more funds will be made available'. If we look at that verse again slowly, and meditatively, we will note that the word **'all'** appears four times and the word **'abound'** twice. If we take the time to meditate on those words we will get a sense of God's plan to fully equip us for <u>every</u> eventuality **for His glory**.

Jesus said, "If you remain in me and **my words** remain in you, ask whatever you wish and it will be given you. This is to my Fathers' glory that you bear much fruit, showing yourselves to be my disciples." (John 15:7,8). So what are **'His words'** on this subject? I think that they are the same words that He spoke to Paul when he was feeling really bad because of his 'thorn in the flesh' (the one the Lord was not taking away), "My grace is sufficient for you, for my power is made perfect in weakness." (2 Corinthians 12:9). However big and deep and far reaching our weakness is, there is sufficient grace to cover it, and Jesus' words encourage us to ask for that grace with faith in our hearts.

So if there is no shortage of supply, how do we make sure that we draw on this supply throughout the day? Yes, you guessed it! I thank Him for that supply in the moment... Thank you Lord for the patience I am needing right now ... thank you for the wisdom for this problem ... thank you for the love I am wanting to express to this person... etc etc... and as I thank Him He pours it out and I receive it. Every drop of grace comes from Him, and the Holy Spirit pours into, with and through the Christ within. My part is to receive and allow that grace to flow out into the world and my situation, through my life, my words and actions.

Activation ...

Today give thanks for whatever aspect of His grace you are needing in each moment, and see how it just flows and flows into your heart and mind, as you lift your gaze to His with an expectant heart.

As Keith Green wrote in 1980 in the first verse of her beautiful song...

'For when your eyes are on this child your grace abounds to me.'[1]

DAY 206 | Thanksgiving that my Supply Point is Jesus

Yesterday we were talking about the fact that there is always sufficient grace for every eventuality, and it occurred to me that 'sufficient' is often the way God is with us. One step at a time, grace for the moment. It's ever flowing but it's never all stored up. Why? Because it's about 'walking' with the Lord, like Enoch. He doesn't give us a backpack full of supplies for the whole of life, or even the whole year, month, or week. He doesn't say "Here are your supplies of grace now off you go." He says "Come let's walk together."

It's the same with guidance. We read in Psalm 119:105, 'Your word is a lamp unto my feet and a light for my path.' A lamp just shows a little way ahead, it's not a searching beam showing us the path miles ahead, but it gives light enough for us to take one more step. I believe the Lord knows that if we had the whole map for the journey and all the provision that we needed too, we would probably soon be walking at some distance from Him, spiritually speaking. God doesn't give us a road map He gives us Himself. He wants to be our Saviour, friend, guide, and provider along the journey.

The Christian life is not a 'religious order', or a 'code of conduct', it's vastly different and many times better than that. It's a relationship with Almighty God. He carries everything that we need for the journey and makes it ours in Christ. Therefore grace for each step comes as we need it, in the form that we need it, from God, through Christ, by the Holy Spirit, and we can be so thankful that that is the way it is.

We have enough of whatever we need in terms of grace, because our provision is tightly linked to His presence. **'For no matter how many promises God has made, they are "Yes" in Christ. And so through Him the "Amen" is spoken by us to the glory of God.'** *(*2 Corinthians 1:20)

What an exciting verse. If I'm with Him I have enough. I have what I need because I am in Christ and He is in me, so God's favour rests upon me. Any promise God has made, I can claim as mine because of Jesus. God says His

"**Yes**" to me because He sees me in Jesus. My "**Amen**" is my shout of faith and agreement, it's my "**so be it**" or, as 'Amen' is written in the Message version (and I love it), it's my "**Oh Yes!**" (Revelation 5:14. The Message).

Activation...

Thank God today that He doesn't treat you like an electric plug in car. Thank Him that you never need to ask "Do I have sufficient charge to get me home, or to 'A', 'B' or 'C'?" You can recharge as you go, because you have the powerful Holy Spirit, the 'dunamis' of God living in you. Today thank God that all the grace that you need in every situation, moment by moment, is yours, because you are in Christ, and the promise is that He 'will supply all your needs **according to His riches in glory in Christ Jesus**.' (Philippians 4:19, NASB).

Give Him heartfelt thanks today that He is with you, He is your heavenly 'supply point' and, even more importantly, He is your friend on the journey.

DAY 207 | Thanksgiving for the 'Much More'

Let's look a little further today into this stupendous scripture that we considered yesterday, that all the promises of God are 'Yes' and 'Amen' in Christ. (2 Corinthians 1:20). Let's look at it in the light of the incredible truth we have been considering over the past couple of days, that there is always sufficient 'grace' for us no matter in what circumstances we find ourselves.

Firstly we need to realise that this word 'grace' has been sadly devalued as it is often used in popular parlance. 'Giving someone grace' can mean giving someone a chance, cutting them some slack, letting some mistake go by without demanding they are punished. We even hear the expression that someone has 'fallen from grace' when they mess up in some way. As if you can fall out of grace by behaving badly. That is when you really need it!!!

For us, in the church, the word grace is also sometimes sadly devalued. We all know that we have been 'saved by grace' not our good behavior, church attendance, or good works but, having been 'saved by grace', we then often speak about grace as if it is a top up thing. "I was doing OK, then I messed up a bit . . ." That is to say I lost my peace/self control/patience/kindness etc. so I needed a 'top up' from God, some 'grace' to help me along. It then feels that 'grace' is a bit like God 'cutting me some slack', overlooking my failures and then giving me a helping hand so I can feel O.K. again.

Oh dear! How sadly the Christian community has underestimated the power that is contained in God's grace, because His grace is not a top up when we are failing; it is nothing less than His empowering presence **the whole time, for the whole of our lives.** No wonder Paul starts **all** His letters without fail with something like, 'Grace to you and peace from God our Father and the Lord Jesus Christ.' See Romans 1:7, 1 Corinthians 1:3, 2 Corinthians 1:2, Galatians 1:3, Ephesians 1:2, Philippians 1:2, Colossians 1:2, 1 Thessalonians 1:1, 2 Thessalonians 1:2, 1 Timothy 1:2, 2 Timothy 1:2, Titus 1:4.

Why did Paul feel compelled to start his letters in this way? I think because he had a revelation of the grace of God that underpinned the whole of salvation; the entire work of Jesus' death, resurrection and ascension on our behalf, and here it is written down for us in Romans 5:17. 'For if, by the trespass of one man, death reigned through that one man, how much more will those who receive God's abundant provision of grace and of the gift of righteousness reign in life through the one man, Jesus Christ.' Jesus' death and resurrection has bought for you and me not just forgiveness and our imputed righteousness, wonderful as that is, but all the abundance of grace that we will ever need in order to reign in life.

We have not just been given a reprieve from our spiritual death, God has 'raised us up with Christ and seated us with him in the heavenly realm in Christ Jesus, in order that in the coming ages (now) he might show the incomparable riches of his grace expressed in his kindness to us in Christ Jesus.' (Ephesians 2:6,7). Or as Paul puts it in his letter to the Galatians, 'I have been crucified with Christ and I no longer live, but Christ lives in me.' (Now that is His empowering presence! That is GRACE.) 'The life I now live in the body, I live by faith in the Son of God who loved me and gave himself for me.' (Galatians 2:20). 'For it is by grace you have been saved, through faith – and this is not from yourselves, it is the gift of God – not by works, so that no one can boast. For we are God's workmanship, created in Christ Jesus to do good works, which God prepared in advance for us to do.' (Ephesians 2:8-10).

This abundance of grace is ours in Christ in order that we will live in a new way from the 'new us', the Christ life within, as a demonstration to the world, and the principalities and powers in the heavenly realms, of what God intended for man when He created Him in the first place.

Activation...

Give thanks today that you have abundant grace for every possible eventuality because 'grace' is nothing less than the empowering presence of the Christ who now lives in you by the Holy Spirit. As you thank the Lord let the truth of Paul's declaration grip your heart and become your declaration also. *"I have been crucified with Christ and I no longer live, but Christ lives in me. The life I now live in the body, I live by faith in the Son of God, who loved me and gave himself for me."* (Galatians 2:20,21).

Your declaration with Paul then becomes your "Amen" to God's "Yes" to you and all you now are, and have, because Jesus lives within.

DAY 208 | Thanksgiving and Reigning in Life

We finished our meditation yesterday with Paul's declaration from his letter to the Galatians that his life was now lived through the indwelling Christ; but this doesn't mean that he wasn't still very aware of his ability to slip back into living out of his old life. He expresses this very poignantly in his letter to the Philippian church in this way: 'Not that I have already obtained all this, or have I already been made perfect, but I press on to take hold of that for which Christ Jesus took hold of me... One thing I do: Forgetting what lies behind and straining towards what is ahead, I press on toward the goal to win the prize for which God has called me heavenward in Christ Jesus.' (Philippians 3:12-14).

Brian Simmons in The Passion Translation writes these verses as, 'I admit that I haven't yet acquired the absolute fullness that I am pursuing, but I run with passion into His abundance so that I may reach the purpose that Christ Jesus has called me to fulfill and wants me to discover. I don't depend on my own strength to accomplish this; however I do have one compelling focus: I forget all of the past as I fasten my heart to the future instead. I run straight for the divine invitation of reaching the heavenly goal and gaining the victory prize through the anointing of Jesus.'

Let's just read that first sentence again very slowly...

'I haven't yet acquired the absolute fullness that I am pursuing, but I run with passion into His abundance so that I may reach the purpose that Christ Jesus has called me to fulfill and wants me to discover.'

Our purpose on the earth is to be increasingly filled with the life of Christ. Our destiny is to live life 'filled' with His life, which is of course (as we wrote in Book 2 Days 163-170) **the** only way to live a life on earth that manifests all the fruit of the Spirit. (Galatians 5:22). It's also the only way we can live out those, 'good works, which God prepared in advance for us to do.' (Ephesians 2:8-10).

In Acts 11:26 we are told that it was in Antioch that the followers of Jesus were first given the name 'Christian'; literally 'a little Christ' or 'little anointed one'. People were clearly 'seeing' a manifestation of Jesus in the lives of these young christians. Certainly Barnabas did. He was sent down to Antioch from the church in Jerusalem to see what was going on. 'When he arrived and saw **the evidence of the grace of God,** he was glad and encouraged them all to remain true to the Lord with all their hearts. He was a good man, full of the Holy Spirit and faith, and a great number of people were brought to the Lord.' (Acts 11:23,24). How wonderful! This is what you and I can carry into the world, **'evidence of the grace of God'**, as we stay full of the Spirit.

We are told in Romans 8:19, AMP. 'For (even the whole) creation (all nature) waits expectantly and longs earnestly for God's sons to be made known [waits for the revealing, the disclosing of their sonship].' The world is waiting to see the Christ life manifested in our lives!!! I wonder if this is the fulfillment of Habakkuk 2:14, – 'For the earth will be filled with the knowledge of the glory of God as the waters cover the sea.' – that there will be a time when God's people so avail themselves of His grace, in every part of their lives, that His glory will be seen by all. I believe so.

Activation...

Today let us join with Paul and ...

'... **run with passion into His abundance so that I may reach the purpose that Christ Jesus has called me to fulfill and wants me to discover.'**

And we can do that – like a child who runs to receive an expected gift from someone they know loves them dearly – **with a heart and a mouth full of 'thanksgiving'.**

DAY 209 | Thanksgiving for our Impossibilities

In the Bible, both Old and New Testaments, we see impossibilities become possible as people follow the leading of their God. We see a fully armed giant slain by a boy without any armour, (1 Samuel 17:45-50); walls around a city fall when there are no battering rams, (Joshua 6:20); water turned to wine, when there are no grapes involved, (John 2:8-10) and of course the dead raised when there is absolutely no defribulators any where to be seen. (John 11:38-43).

The miraculous, or the 'impossible' happening, is a regular feature in the life of God's people, because our God, who created all things by the power of His word, is more than happy to break the rules of nature and the universe for His people and for His glory. We have a faith that assumes there will be miracles.

One of the most famous impossibilities was when Mary was told that, although a virgin, she was to have a baby and so was her barren, very old cousin Elizabeth. The Angel Gabriel explains, "The Holy Spirit will come upon you and the power of the Most High will overshadow you. So the holy one to be born will be called the Son of God." He then concludes with those famous words, **"For nothing is impossible with God"**. (Luke 1:35-37).

The other time that we hear that God can make the 'impossible' 'possible', is when Jesus was talking with the disciples about how hard it was for the rich to enter the Kingdom of heaven. They asked, "Who then can be saved?" and Jesus replies, "With man this is impossible, but not with God; **all things are possible with God**". (Mark 10:26,27). The truth is we have a God who can make a heavy axe head float, (2 Kings 6:6), make the sun stand still, (Joshua 10:12-14), and raise His Son from the dead after Satan did his worst. (Matthew 28:5-10).

For many of us (myself included) the measure of our faith, that the impossible can happen in our day, can be somewhat depleted. There are people we have prayed for, and things that we have asked God to do, and we have not seen what we wanted to see. We are however living in days when God is drawing us back to believe that our God is the God of the impossible. We hear of people of other faiths having dreams and seeing visions of Jesus; we hear of healings and miracles in areas of the world where there is no real health care, and we hear increasing numbers of testimonies in our own country of conversions and healings.

Before He ascended, Jesus said, "And these signs will accompany those who believe: In my Name they will drive out demons; they will speak in new tongues; they will pick up snakes with their hands; and when they drink deadly poison, it will not hurt them at all; they will place their hands on sick people, and they will get well." (Mark 16:17,18). And so we have a choice like Joshua, Caleb and the other ten spies did, recorded for us in Numbers 13:26-33. When faced with the size of the giants and walled cities in the Promised Land, their responses to their problem (summarised beautifully for us in a children's song we use to sing) was – 'ten said "NO", two said "GO". Ten looked at the size of their problem, two looked at the size of their God and the promises that He had made them.

Activation ...

Today if you are discouraged, don't revise your theology to fit your experience, but thank God for your impossibilities. If we didn't have impossibilities, (or impossible people!), in our lives we would not be challenged to seek Him for more.

As you pray for the people you know and love who seem oblivious to the Lord, or those who appear to be like 'walled cities'; and as you pray for the 'giant' miracles that you need to see in your life, or the lives of your family and community, thank God that He is calling us back to being a people who see His divine interventions in our everyday life. Take every opportunity to dig deep and find a faith story in the Word to feed on and thank God that He is still **the God of the impossible!**

And let us thank Him together that He has not finished with us yet!!

DAY 210 | Thanksgiving is more Relational than Transactional

If you have been journeying with us through books One and Two in this series, you will have noticed that one of the things that has come out of our meditations on thanksgiving is that thanksgiving is a living dynamic thing not a formula, contract, or procedure, or even a rule that we must follow. Indeed, when you think about it, it is something about which we have free choice every day. Shall I be actively thankful or not? Our study in Romans 1 reminded us that things start to go wrong when people decide not to be, or neglect being, thankful, and that we all do have that freedom to choose.

When you consider the human arena, our thanksgiving is always directed at people – it is relational even when it is for an item, or a service. I thank you for the box of chocolates, the lift you gave me, the meal you made for me. Even when it is for something like modern medicine, I can express my thankfulness for the people who had the knowledge, skill and dedication to discover and perfect these things, and to those providing me with them.

What does that say to me? Well maybe it adds something to Psalm 100:4 'Enter his gates with thanksgiving and his courts with praise; give thanks to him and praise his name.' Sometimes we apply that to the start of a church service, or worship time, but what if it is speaking of our daily, morning by morning, when I wake up, moment by moment relationship with the Lord, as I live my daily, normal, up and down life? I think that we are beginning to see that our friendship, our relationship with the Lord flows with and is fueled by thanksgiving.

Sometimes a contrast helps to clarify this, like white chalk on a blackboard. Consider the Children of Israel going through the wilderness. They did a lot of complaining. Now humanly speaking you could say there was a lot to complain about; hot sand, water shortage, lack of food, lack of variety of food, enemies circling to attack etc. But whilst understandable at a human level, complaining did not do them a lot of good. Why? Because it obscured their vision of how good God had been to them and the mighty things He had done for them, and was still doing for them. It therefore spoilt their relationship with Him.

God is so good, kind and patient that it did NOT stop God miraculously providing for them, but they were not enjoying His friendship, or even, at times, some of the things He was doing for them. If they could have chosen thanksgiving, even in their difficulties, they would still have been provided for, and in addition they would have enjoyed a great relationship with the Lord, who was both Father and Mother to them throughout this time. Its rather like human parenting, Mum and Dad can provide all that is needed for their kids, but beyond that, what a difference either complaining or thanksgiving makes to the pleasure of the parent child relationship.

We too have problems big and small in our daily lives. It's not difficult to find something in life that is difficult, uncomfortable, scary, or plain horrible; things about which we might feel tempted to grumble and complain. It is then worth reminding ourselves that thanksgiving is a very significant way to express and grow our faith. I face a problem, maybe a bill, I can pray "Please help me God", and that is good and God listens and responds.

However, if in the midst of that prayer I also say, "thank you Lord that you are my Jehovah Jireh, my provider", "thank you Lord that Psalm 23 says 'nothing will I lack' because I have made you my shepherd", and I continue in that vein, by the time I have finished, there is not just a whole lot more faith going round in my heart for God's action and intervention in my problem, but I will also find that I am in a closer relationship with Him.

Activation...

Remind yourself today that your thanksgiving, your decision to express your gratitude to God is not a transaction whereby you get what you want from the Lord, but it is an expression of your connection with His heart of love for you. You can even thank Him that the choice to give thanks in all circumstances (1Thessalonians 5:18) which, on occasions sounds like a big ask, actually draws you into a deeper relationship with Him based on your appreciation of all He is and has done, and all He will do for you. It brings you right into His courts, His holy presence every time.

DAY 211 | Thanksgiving for Spiritual Hunger

I've always assumed that when Jesus said, "Blessed are the poor in spirit for theirs is the Kingdom of heaven." (Matthew 5:3), that He was talking about an awareness of spiritual poverty that leads a person to salvation. I am thinking today that it is more than that, and that in fact Jesus meant it, like the other beatitudes, as a principle for life.

I personally don't like feeling inadequate. I don't think many of us do. It feels uncomfortable not to feel 'on top of my game' as it were. We like to feel that we have the resources to cope with the situations in which we find ourselves, physically, mentally, emotionally and of course spiritually. Feeling 'poor' in spirit therefore, doesn't sit well with some of the other truths that we have been thanking God for, like the fact that there is grace abounding for all our needs.

If I feel a sense of deficit in any area, I am less likely to feel content and happy let alone 'Blessed', and yet that is what Jesus said. "Blessed are the poor in spirit, for theirs is the Kingdom of Heaven." So this morning 'a penny' dropped as three scriptures came together for me and I think I understood a little more about this amazing principle of spiritual life, about which Jesus was talking.

I was reading from Psalm 36:7-9, 'How priceless is your unfailing love! Both high and low among men find refuge in the shadow of your wings. They feast on the abundance of your house; you give them to drink of the river of your delights. For with you is the fountain of life; in your light we see light.' This is not about status; both high and low (all 'the children of men' in the NASB) can come, it's about **hunger**, and they can come and seek refuge in the Lord and find themselves in a spiritually rich place where they can 'feast on abundance.'

It reminds me of the line in Mary's song, "The **hungry** He has filled with good things but has sent the rich away empty" (Luke1:53). It also reminds me of the Lord's invitation through Isaiah. "Come, all you who are thirsty, come to the waters; and you who have no money, come buy and eat! Come, buy wine and milk without money or cost . . . Listen to me and eat what is good. And your soul will delight in the richest of fare." (Isaiah 55:1,2).

The sense of hunger is such an important one for survival naturally. It drives us to look for food and to then eat it. If someone has no appetite, it can be a sign that all is not well. Sometimes when people reach the end of their life, they will even stop wanting food. It is as if their body has decided it is time to go. The 'normal' is for our body to regularly crave an intake of food, the fuel to keep us functioning properly.

As in the natural, so it is in the spiritual. If we have no spiritual hunger we can assume that something is not right with our spiritual life. We need that spiritual food described in Psalm 36 at regular intervals and not just as an annual, or even a weekly binge. It means that I can feel very blessed, but then very hungry again within a day, or a short period of time. I can experience the overflowing grace of God in one minute but then be aware of my spiritual poverty the next, when another challenge or situation comes where I am feeling my lack of peace, or wisdom, or resource.

We do just need to note here that this word 'blessed' is not the stained glass window kind of 'blessed'; it's not the image of a saint sitting with a halo and some sheep at his feet. Brian Simmonds in The Passion Translation tells us that the Aramaic word that Jesus would probably have used, 'Toowayhon', implies 'great happiness, prosperity, or enrichment, abundant goodness and delight'.

Any feelings of spiritual poverty is not necessarily because I haven't known the Lord's blessing but perhaps because I have, and I want more. It's because as I travel through the day fresh challenges have come, causing me to become aware of my 'spiritual poverty'. I then become hungry for more of Him and return to the fountain to drink deeply once again. Then I find myself truly 'blessed' for more of the Kingdom of Heaven becomes mine.

Activation ...

Now you know that you can thank the Lord every time you feel that sense of being 'poor in spirit'. It's your **hunger** pangs for more of His Kingdom to be released in you, and so you know that you are going to be truly 'blessed'.

DAY 212 | Spiritual Hunger and Thirst

Yesterday we were thinking about how our personal sense of spiritual poverty could be a blessing, in that it was the spiritual equivalent of hunger pangs, causing us to go to the Lord for sustenance. Psalm 36, from which we quoted yesterday, is something of an Old Testament equivalent to the beatitudes, 'Blessed are those who hunger and thirst after righteousness, for they will be filled (or satisfied).' (Matthew 5:6).

The psalmist begins that psalm with a lament, not about personal spiritual poverty, but about the state of the world and the wickedness that he sees all around. He writes of the wicked, 'there is no fear of God before his eyes . . ., he flatters himself too much to detect or hate his sin. The words of his mouth are wicked and deceitful; he has ceased to be wise and to do good . . . he commits himself to a sinful course and does not reject what is wrong.' (Psalm 36:1-4).

Now I know that there are many good and kind people all around us, but I do believe that it is hard to live as a Christian in today's world and not become vexed by the kinds of things we are seeing and hearing about day by day. There is a constant barrage of information about things happening in the world, that should never, never happen given the beauty of our created world and the magnificence of mankind as the crown of God's creation. However, as C.S. Lewis reminds us, 'mankind is noble but fallen'.

We know that many things are amplified by the media, but nevertheless it is grievous that so many people are living lives well below who God destined them to be, and to become, in His love for them. Furthermore it can often feel as if, in our world, right and wrong have been reversed and that the devil has so deceived people that they don't even long for goodness and righteousness anymore, nor for the God who made them.

We can vex ourselves about these things. We can find ourselves recounting things that we have read about, or dwelling on the evil in the world, both in our own minds and to others, but we know that doesn't actually change anything, or help us. King David's advice is, 'Do not fret because of evil men or be envious of those who do wrong ... do not fret when men succeed in their ways, ... refrain from anger ... do not fret – it leads only to evil.' What wisdom for our day, written fifteen hundred years ago!!

Instead he says, 'trust in the Lord and do good ... delight yourself in the Lord ... commit your way to the Lord ... be still before the Lord and wait patiently for Him ... ' (Psalm 37:1-8). And then we read back in Psalm 36 'Your love, O Lord, reaches to the heavens, your faithfulness to the skies. Your righteousness is like the mighty mountains, your justice like the great deep ... How priceless is your unfailing love! Both high and low among men find refuge in the shadow of your wings. They feast on the abundance of your house; you give them drink from your river of delights. For with you is the fountain of life; in your light we see light.' (Psalm 36:7-9).

God loves that we are grieved about the state of the world, but not that we rail about it, fret ourselves, moan and complain about it, or recount to each other how awful it is. He loves that we hunger and thirst after righteousness and He loves it even more if that hunger causes us to seek Him, trust and delight in Him, commit our way to Him, and wait on Him, again and again. His promise is that we shall be 'satisfied', or 'filled'. So let us thank Him that we feel His grief over the state of His world, and let that grief drive us to Him as we hunger and thirst after righteousness.

Activation ...

Thank the Lord today that there is somewhere really good to go when you are feeling vexed about it all. Come into His sanctuary, under the shadow of His wings and, yes, feast on His goodness and righteousness and kindness. In His light you too will see light. You will see situations and people the way He sees them, and be able to speak to them with hope and faith in your heart.

Remember that this word 'blessed' means great happiness, prosperity or enrichment, abundant goodness and delight. So when the enemy puts his wares on display, let your hunger and thirst for righteousness drive you deeper into the arms the Lord. Thank Him that He welcomes you and that you will then find yourself richly blessed – 'satisfied' with His goodness.

DAY 213 | Thanksgiving – a Great Faith Fertilizer

Faith is a great mystery. I don't mean 'saving faith' but the faith that moves mountains, or that sees healings and miracles. We know that it is God's power that heals, but even when Jesus had felt that power leave Him for healing He said to the woman who touched Him, "Daughter, **your faith** has healed you." (Mark 5:30-34). He also said to two blind men who came for healing, "According to **your faith** will it be done to you." (Matthew 9:29). Another statement that He made in Nazareth, linking His power to faith, can be a little unnerving. Remember that in Nazareth Jesus was not able to do many miracles, and He was therefore amazed at their 'lack of faith'. (Mark 6:6).

Jesus makes it clear that faith is involved in releasing the power of God into our world, but I feel more in the company of the young boy's father who, when told that, "Everything is possible for him who believes", replied to Jesus, "I do believe; help me overcome my unbelief." (Mark 9:24). Clearly there is something that we need to do to release the power of God and it is this somewhat illusive thing described as 'having faith'!

If you're a gardener you will know the difference a good dose of fertilizer makes. The farmer near us applies the fertilizer when the first shoots begin to appear, long **before** the fruit appears. It struck me that thanksgiving is a lot like that fertilizer, it feeds my faith and grows it till there is a harvest to reap, but it needs to be applied **before** the fruit actually appears.

If when the first shoots of the 'crop' came through the farmer thinks, "Well that's not what I am looking for I won't bother now to look after that crop.", we would wonder about his judgement. We would expect that seeing the green shoots he would feel encouraged that the crop hasn't died, and so he would feed those shoots and care for them until the fruit appears.

It seems to me that it can be a little like this with our praying 'in faith'. We are looking for answers to prayer. It could be someone's conversion or some money that we need; perhaps healing in some part of our, or someone else's body or mind, and very little seems to be happening. Sometimes things even seem to get worse. At other times, however some small thing happens; equivalent to those green shoots, but because it is far short of what we have been praying for we get disappointed and may be even say to ourselves, "Yet again I didn't have enough faith to see the breakthrough."

What if instead of getting discouraged and giving up we said to ourselves "There's a shoot here"? And then said, "Thank you God for this little beginning; this small sign that there is some life here". What if we stop saying, "this is just a shoot but there is no fruit here"? What if we let our thanksgiving be the fertilizer that feeds our faith causing it to grow?

So how does this work out in practice? We meet a friend or neighbour for whom we have been praying, and we don't 'lead them to the Lord', but they do share with us about the child, (or parent) they are worried about and we offer to pray. We don't get that brown envelope through the post, with the money that we need, but the car does miraculously pass the MOT! The lump we are praying about doesn't disappear, but the scan shows that it has shrunk slightly. These, combined with the knowledge of God's character and promises are the green shoots for which we can intentionally give thanks, and thereby feed our faith.

In every example of the miraculous in the bible, faith was expressed by simply coming to Jesus, calling out to Him, touching Him, or asking Him for what was needed. Turning to Him with thanksgiving in our hearts for any 'green shoots' is a way of 'coming to Jesus' and expressing our mustard seed faith. It is saying, "Thank you Lord, that's wonderful and can I have more?"

Activation ...

The good news is that Jesus did heal the boy of the father who said "I do believe. Help me overcome my unbelief."(Mark 9:25,26). Jesus responds to our honesty and He is happy that we are on a journey to grow our faith. So make sure you look for the green shoots and take every opportunity to put on the fertilizer of thanksgiving, so that you will thereby grow in your faith and reap a harvest.

DAY 214 | Thanksgiving a Weapon against Taking Offense!

We know that there is offense in the gospel. Peter tells us that Jesus is, 'a stone of stumbling, and a rock of offence, *even to them* which stumble at the word,' (1 Peter 2:8, AV). As far as the Lord is concerned, however, He doesn't want offence given or taken by those of us within His family, so Paul prays for the Philippian church that as their love abounds they will be, 'sincere and without offence till the day of Christ;' (Philippians 1:10, AV).

Jesus himself said, 'It is impossible but that offences will come; but woe *unto him*, through whom they come!' (Luke 17:1, AV). It's important therefore that we don't cause another to be offended. However today I want to reflect on the importance of not taking offence ourselves, and indeed even more importantly, that we don't get offended with God. I think poor John the Baptist had this challenge when he was in prison. We can tell this from Jesus response to him when he sent his disciples to Jesus to ask, "Are you the Expected One, or shall we look for someone else?" (He was clearly having an issue with the fact that Jesus wasn't getting him out of prison).

Jesus tells John's disciples to, "Go and report to John what you hear and see: *the* BLIND RECEIVE SIGHT *and the lame walk, the* lepers are cleansed *and the* deaf hear, *the* dead are raised *and the* POOR HAVE THE GOSPEL PREACHED TO THEM." (no mention then, of captives being released from prison, as in Isaiah 42:7?) So Jesus then tells them to say to John, "And blessed is he who does not take offense at me." (Matthew 11:4-6, NASB). That is to say, something may feel offensive, but offence doesn't have to be taken.

You may have noticed that I have been using a lot of AV quotes today, and that is because later versions of the bible don't use the word 'offence'. They speak rather of things that cause us to stumble, which is fair enough as the Oxford English dictionary defines 'an offence' as 'a stumbling block'. I think however that 'offence' is a more appropriate word for us today. I may stumble over something because I haven't noticed it was there, i.e.

I am a passive victim of the situation, but if I 'take offence', I am an active participant. I play an active part in my own stumbling.

We were in a situation once which cost us a great deal and it felt like the Lord had forgotten us. A good friend gave me a text, 'Great peace have they which love thy law and nothing shall offend them.' (Psalm 119:165, AV). I knew then I had a choice whether I got offended, not just with my fellow Christians, but with God Himself. I knew then that I couldn't afford to be offended with God, I needed His friendship, and His peace too much.

None of us like to be thought of as offensive, or easily offended, but this morning I felt that the Lord was saying that when there is a risk of us 'taking offence at something or someone, we can 'go on the offensive' – the weapon of choice? – 'Thanksgiving'. When we are feeling at risk of being offended, like John the Baptist, we can choose not to 'take' offence and give thanks instead. In this way we bullet proof ourselves against the fiery darts of the enemy, who wants to encourages us into self pity, resentment or even anger – to be offended, which will undoubtedly undermine our 'faith.'

If we don't take offence, then the devil can't cause division, or get us to have a 'stand-off' with the Lord. Thanksgiving enables us to go on the **offensive, and** we can cause the devil to 'stumble' in his attempts to derail us. Offence can be given but it also has to be taken, and so thanksgiving helps to stop us from becoming offended by our fellow Christians or by God.

Activation . . .

As we give thanks in these difficult situations we keep our connection with the Lord strong. In this way the wedge which the enemy would seek to drive between us and the Lord is neutralised.

Giving glory to God is something that offends the enemy when he is tempting us to either give or take offence. It sends him packing, so let's do it and enjoy the freedom that it will bring us.

DAY 215 | Thanksgiving that Helps us to Walk in Peace!

Do you ever look at the diary and think, 'I'm not sure how I'm going to manage all the demands, or find the time needed for everything I need to do this week!' Sometimes when we look ahead at a busy week, we can rush into things trying to 'get ahead' or 'stay on top' of things. Well, there is something that the Lord wants to teach us about walking with Him and the, 'unforced rhythms of grace.' (Matthew 11:29, The Message).

Without doubt our lives today are crammed. There are so many possibilities for our precious time, things that we have to do, things that we want to do, and things that we feel we 'ought' to do, 'should do', or 'must do'. It is so very easy to overstretch ourselves and then feel very out of sync with our own bodies, but more importantly, out of sync with the Lord. Life can feel like a gallop through a forest – going far too fast whilst narrowly avoiding trees and obstacles, rather than a walk along a hillside with time to stop and enjoy the view.

Enoch 'walked with God for three hundred years', (Genesis 5:22-24), but then he didn't have constant demands coming at him via our modern technology, nor the transport that would have enabled him to travel from one place to another, from one demand to another, in minutes. So how do we 'walk with God' in our world today?

Rushing at things, I have discovered to my cost, is never the answer. I make mistakes, forget things, have to do things over again, and even if I do take short cuts and finish something quickly so that I can move onto the next thing, it feels less than satisfactory. There is always that feeling at the end of the day that I 'made it' but I could have done lots of things a lot better. To be able to 'walk' through a day at a steady pace, giving time and attention to people and things, can be so much more satisfying.

Thanking the Lord at the beginning of the day, for that day and all that is going to fill our day, slows us down in our heads. It stops us from rushing at life allowing us to 'make more haste, less speed' – as the old adage goes. Taking time to pause and thank the Lord **during** the day, for the known and unknowns of that day, also enables us to hear His wisdom, His voice saying, " leave that now", "trust me for that", " get on with that phone call now", "ask ... to help you with that" etc.etc.

Taking a moment, and deliberately thanking the Lord for His presence with me, keeps me travelling through the day at His pace, which can often feel so much slower than the pace at which I think I should be moving. Taking those moments to pause and thank Him, especially when I feel under pressure, enables me to move at what is ultimately a more productive and fruitful pace.

Even more importantly, thanksgiving keeps me close to the Lord, so that I am not derailed by the unexpected demand, or interruption in the day, which is always a challenge if the day already feels over full. Taking a moment to thank God when an unexpected demand arises, allows the Holy Spirit to remind me that, 'as your day, so shall your strength, your rest *and security, be.*' (Deuteronomy 33:25, AMP). That same verse in the NASB is translated, 'According to your days, so will your leisurely walk be.' I think that is a good one for me – may be for you too?

Activation...

This week, remember to start your days **and** sprinkle them with those pauses, those moments of thanksgiving, and I think you will be surprised at how much you achieve when you walk with Lord at His pace. He says to us again and again, 'Come to Me. Get away with Me and you'll recover your life...walk with Me-watch how I do it. Learn the unforced rhythms of grace. I won't lay anything heavy or ill-fitting on you. Keep company with me and you'll learn to live freely and lightly.' (Matthew 11:28,29, The Message).

DAY 216 | Thanksgiving and Saying 'NO'!

Yesterday we were looking at how pausing to give thanks to the Lord at regular intervals throughout our day can help us to keep in step with the Lord and to accomplish all that the day holds, at His pace, and in 'peace'. Nevertheless I am sure that we are all aware how easy it is to overload the system, to agree to too many things, even good things, and find ourselves living with 'hurry sickness' because there are just not enough hours in the day, even if we do keep thanking the Lord for His presence and help.

I think one reason why some of us find walking through our days in peace, at the Lord's pace, eludes us, is our difficulty with saying 'No'. We say yes to things that are not part of the Lord's plan for us, and then we find ourselves overstretched and rushing through things that are important to Him, like that conversation with a neighbour. We can find ourselves too busy to live out the life that we, in our heart, would want to live. So today we are going to consider how thanksgiving can actually help us to say "No".

"Wow", I hear someone ask, "Are Christians allowed to say 'No'?" Well yes! Of course we are allowed. We're even supposed to say 'no' to the devil, to temptation, to breaking the law etc. The main biblical command is that we are not to accompany our 'no', or our 'yes' with swearing (Matthew 5:36,37). Sometimes we can feel bad about saying 'no', because we think and feel that it is not what Jesus would want. We hear His teaching, 'And if someone wants to sue you and take your tunic, let him have your cloak as well … Give to the one who asks you, and do not turn away from the one who wants to borrow from you.' (Matthew 5:40-42), and from this we can wrongly draw the conclusion that He always wants us to say 'Yes'.

The thing that we need to understand is that every 'yes' has a cost that will result in us saying a 'no' to something else. By saying my 'yes' to various things I am going to be saying an saying an implicit 'no' to other things. Put simply the problem is that if I find it hard to say 'no', the result will be that I will say 'yes' to the things and people that shout at me the loudest, and I may therefore end up saying a tacit 'no' to other things that may even be more important, but that don't shout at me quite so loudly.

If I want to spend an hour at the gym, that time is no longer available to decorate my house. Spending time helping my neighbour, will mean less time for the gym. There is a cost to every 'yes'. Every time I agree to do someone a favour, even a small one, I need to reckon that there will be a cost, and not just assume that I can absorb it into the day. Every 'yes' needs to be realistically informed about the cost in terms of time and energy.

If I can pause and give thanks to the Lord when I am faced with a decision about how I spend some time I will in fact be beginning a conversation with Him, and giving myself some time to consider my options. If instead of reacting with a fast 'yes' or 'no', I say "Lord I thank you for this request", or for this opportunity or even, "Lord I thank you for this decision that I have to make. I invite you Holy Spirit to lead and guide me now", I am more likely to hear the Holy Spirit's whisper or nudge. If I'm not sure, taking some time can be a great help. Saying 'I will think about it' is OK and can be said in various ways, but let thanksgiving be your 'pause button' that helps you to stay connected to the Holy Spirit.

So, what if with hindsight I've committed myself to too much? Well the Lord does care, and He will take care, but He also wants us to learn. So if pausing and giving thanks for a demand or a request, before we say yes, can really help us to slow the pace of life and reduce 'overload', giving thanks can also help us to walk through overly busy days with the Lord, even if we feel that it is our own fault that we have agreed to too much. Giving thanks helps me to stay in harmony with the Lord and therefore in peace. It frees me to cancel things, to ask for help, to slim down a task or leave a conversation earlier than I normally would.

Activation . . .

Give thanks today before you respond to different requests that come your way. Turn your heart to the Lord and as you do, let the Holy Spirit help and guide you into a peaceful walk in all your decision making. And how about giving the Holy Spirit your 'to do list'! See how He leads and guides and gets it worked out as He shows you His priorities for your life? It could be fun, and certainly it will be a faith building exercise!

DAY 217 | Thanksgiving that helps to Protect me from getting Sidetracked by Rules

Yesterday we were reflecting on the role of 'thanksgiving' as it helps me to say my 'No' to things that are too much, or do not seem to be what God wants me to do. This opens up a fresh vista on the things that we have been considering over the last few months. We have been seeing that there are many way in which thanksgiving helps us to move forward, grow in faith and stay in the flow with the Lord and His Spirit, but in helping us to say 'No' thanksgiving also becomes a means of protection and a defense.

Today we are going to look at another way in which thanksgiving can protect us. This is from getting sidetracked, deceived or bogged down in 'rules' and 'laws' that sound spiritual but aren't. In Paul's first letter to Timothy, he writes about people who are forbidding marriage and also telling believers to abstain from certain foods. (1 Timothy 4:1-5). Clearly Paul (and the Holy Spirit) are indicating that these two teachings are wrong. So let's notice how important thanksgiving can be in negotiating our way through the questions that face us today about what is right/wrong, good/bad, ok/not ok, for us Christians in our walk with God.

Paul writes, 'For everything God created is good, and nothing is to be rejected if it is received with thanksgiving . . .' Twice in two verses Paul repeats the importance of receiving things with thanksgiving. It would therefore seem that a heart and practice of thanksgiving is likely to be a great aid in helping us to see the wood for the trees; to separate walking in a way that pleases God in righteousness, from getting sidetracked by religious practices that appear to be pious and godly but actually cut across the character, heart and goodness of God.

When Paul was writing his letters the early church was already experiencing some people trying to put rules in place that would take from the simplicity of the 'Good News' – the Gospel. The issues can be summed up in the difference between 'Rules' and 'Relationship'. Because we love Him we keep His commandments, (John 14:23). But restored relationship is salvation by grace through faith. This gives us an ongoing relationship whereby we are able to cry 'Abba Father'. The life of Christ within us is at the core and this is then followed by a life of growing in the fruit of the indwelling Spirit and doing works that arise from faith.

Jesus said, "If you love me, you will obey what I command. And I will ask the Father, and he will give you another Counselor to be with you forever- the Spirit of truth." (John 14:15,16). The Holy Spirit is our help and guide both in discerning truth and in keeping in step with the Lord and obeying His commands. He will 'remind us' of Jesus words, (John 14:25), and He will 'guide us into all truth.' And Jesus said "He will bring glory to me by taking from what is mine and making it known to you." (John 16:13, 14).

Thanksgiving, as we have previously written, helps us to pause, listen and 'hear' what the Holy Spirit is saying to us. Knowing the Lord's will in any situation then becomes about 'Relationship' not 'Rules. Thanksgiving will then be a great aid to bring me back to that core; my relationship with my good and loving Lord. A heart of thanksgiving will be powerful in reminding me who God is, what He likes and who I am as His beloved child. Then I am likely to be in a much better place to discern the practical will of God in daily life and to have the wisdom to 'keep His commandments', and to not get sidetracked by the wrong sort of religious practices.

Activation ...

When you are next confronted with a teaching, doctrine or practice, about which you are unsure, 'Give Thanks' to the Holy Spirit for His presence and wisdom to discern the right path and He will help you and lead you into all truth. Give thanks in expectation that He will help you seek the truth as you open up God's word, the Bible, or talk with trusted Christian friends. As you give thanks your relationship with Him will grow and you will receive wisdom and revelation. You will be living from that relationship and not from man made rules or doctrines.

DAY 218 | Thanksgiving in Times of Trouble

We have been considering how 'giving thanks' keeps us walking in step with the Lord. It keeps us connected in faith with Him, through busy times, overstretched times, and it keeps us in good relationship with Him through those times of deciding what is the right way for us, in the face of some strong opinions all around us. So, in case that seems like we are saying that everyday will then be 'a walk in the park', today we are looking at how thanksgiving helps us when we are making a mess of the day, or when the difficulties come and it feels overwhelming.

In Psalm 37:23 (AV), we read that, 'the steps of a *good* man are ordered by the Lord: and He delighteth in his way.'. The Amplified Bible expands 'delighteth' to [He busies Himself with his every step]. That, for me, shifts the sense of God being somewhere 'out there' being pleased with me as I try to walk through today aright, to God watching intently, being intimately involved, and even ordering my steps, for His glory.

In the very next verse David declares his confidence that even though this 'good' or 'god fearing' man may himself fall, or stumble it will not be a disaster. Why? 'for the Lord upholds him with His hand.' I so love that verse. How wonderful and what a relief to know that we have such a faithful God; that, in our mistakes and stumblings, He is not 'giving us marks out of ten'. Nor is He declaring 'You have failed to walk with Me today in a proper fashion'. No! He is putting out His Mighty Hand to hold us, just as He did to Peter when he began to sink in his epic adventure, when he got out of the boat onto a stormy sea. (Matthew 14:28-32).

Turning to the Amplified Bible again, we read that this 'good man', 'though he falls, he shall not be utterly cast down, for the Lord grasps his hand in support *and* upholds him.' (Psalm 37:24). Clearly the original words used here denote that, when we are in trouble, our God is very proactive on our behalf. He grasps us, letting us know that He is right with us in the mixture of highs and lows that life is. It reminds me of the promises in Isaiah 43:2,3, 'When you pass through the waters, **I will be with you**; and when you pass through the rivers, they will not sweep over you. When you walk through the fire, you will not be burned; the flames will not set you ablaze. For I am the Lord your God . . .' We again read that the Lord wants to have an intimate relationship with us by specifically declaring '**I will be with you**' in those times of danger.

This is so important because so many of us feel that, when trouble comes, either 'this is happening because I have done something wrong', or else 'it seems like the Lord has left me today otherwise why would it all be going wrong?' We have a perfectionist view of walking with God that doesn't include Him walking with us through our troubled times, or of even allowing there to be troubled times. A far better position to take up is that of, 'Even though I walk through the valley . . . I will fear no evil, for **you are with me**; your rod and your staff they comfort (strengthen) me.' (Psalm 23:4).

Interestingly David uses the personal pronoun 'you' here for the first time in this psalm as he expresses his absolute confidence that **when**, not **if**, he is in trouble the Lord will most definitely be there helping him through. The antidote therefore to feeling 'I must have done something wrong', or to the thought that 'God is a million miles away', is to thank Him that His promises still stand. To thank Him that He is, and will be with me in the valley, the flood, or the fire. That, even if the trouble is of my own making, He is faithful and will stay with me and help me through it.

Thanksgiving helps me to ward off the accusations and insinuations of the evil one. It helps me to grasp His hand as He reaches out to grasp mine and uphold me. Thanksgiving that He is with me and for all His promises to help me in trouble, enables me to walk with Him and declare with David, 'He makes my feet like hinds' feet [able to stand firmly or make progress on the dangerous heights of testing and trouble]; He sets my feet securely upon my high places . . . Your right hand has held me up; your gentleness *and* condescension have made me great.' (Psalm 18:33,35. AMP).

Activation . . .

Thank Him today for all the times He has 'grasped' your hand when you were stumbling, and then thank Him for His gentle but strong faithfulness. Know assuredly that He will never let you go!

DAY 219 | Thanksgiving that Entwines my Heart with His

Over the past few days we have been looking at the importance of thanksgiving when it comes to 'keeping in step' with the Lord, through busy times, overstretched times, challenging times, and through times of trouble. Yesterday I came across some verses in another psalm that seem to gather all those thoughts and take them to another level. They are from Psalm 25, verses 4 and 5, and I am going to write them out from The Passion Translation.

> 'Lord, direct me throughout my journey so I can experience your plans for my life. Reveal the life paths that are pleasing to you. Escort me along the way; take me by the hand and teach me. For you are the God of my increasing salvation; I have wrapped my heart into yours!'

That last beautiful phrase is more commonly translated as, 'For you I wait all the day.' (NASB.) This brings us back to the notion of 'waiting on the Lord' from Isaiah 40:31 which we explored on Days 191, 192 and 193. We shared our belief that thanksgiving was an essential part of 'waiting on the Lord'. I now sense that the Holy Spirit is saying that this 'waiting' is not just for those times when we feel weary, physically emotionally or spiritually; it's not just something whereby I can pause, 'renew my strength' and then just carry on running or walking because I'm back to 'full steam' ... **'waiting on the Lord' is in fact to be my 'posture' for the whole of life.**

In the footnotes to Psalm 25, in The Passion Translation, we read that the Hebrew word most commonly translated as 'wait' is qavah, which also means 'to tie together by twisting', 'to entwine', or 'to wrap tightly' and so this is why the translator has chosen to use the phrase 'I have wrapped my heart into yours', in place of 'for you I wait all the day.' We can see how, thanksgiving which is an essential ingredient in our 'waiting on the Lord', actually causes our heart to be 'entwined' with the Lord's heart. His desire is, and has always been, for us His people to be walking very closely with Him, inseparably linked with Him at the deepest level of our being, throughout all the ups and downs and challenges of life.

Is this the 'deep calling to deep' that we read of in Psalm 42:7? Was this Daniel's secret in finding the place in God where, 'He reveals deep and hidden things'? Certainly Daniel talks of that entwined place where the Lord was able to share with Him the interpretation of a significant dream for a mighty king? If so I'm in!! Interestingly Daniel goes straight on to link thanksgiving with the wisdom he has received. He says, "I thank and praise you, O God of my father's: You have given me wisdom and power." (Daniel 2:22,23).

In the Song of Songs we get a glimpse into the heart of God for the kind and quality of relationship that God is looking for. Remember we are called 'the bride of the Lamb (Christ)' (Revelation 21:9. NASB). The Shulammite writes 'He has brought me to *his* banquet hall, and His banner over me is love.' (Song of Songs 2:4. NASB.) Now that is close! The simplicity of thanksgiving, is the key to a deep and close friendship with the King of Kings, and it brings me to the place where I can say, "His banner over ME is love."

Activation . . .

Let thanksgiving be the key to keeping you in that posture of 'waiting on Him' throughout the day, the key to keeping your heart 'entwined' with His.

Then with your heart filled with gratitude and your mouth filled with thanksgiving, stay close and see what 'hidden things' He may want to whisper in your ear, giving you, like Daniel, wisdom and power in all your circumstances.

DAY 220 | Thanksgiving and the Battle Within

We have been sharing about the joy and benefit of learning to 'wait' on the Lord as a lifestyle; of finding our strength renewed as we journey through the day, learning to catch the thermals of His love. This is described in the Passion Translation as, 'wrapping our hearts in His', (Psalm 25:5). This gives us a great defense when life presses in on us, causing us to lose our peace. There are times however, when the things that stop my heart from being 'entwined' with the Lord's heart are 'within' my own heart. In other words it's not always the external pressures of life, 'the giants in the land', that weigh me down and cause the weariness, but the battles generated from my own thoughts and feelings.

Do you ever have a day like that, when you're battling in your inner world? Those doubts, fears, feelings of condemnation, grumpiness, even discouragement and hopelessness? Then what about feelings of envy, anger, criticism and judgement . . . ? The list is endless, and it is when this 'battle for the mind' is raging that we can feel most disconnected from the Lord. Far from feeling that our heart is entwined with His, we feel that He Himself would probably not want to be anywhere near us! At these times I find the imagery from Psalm 24 especially helpful, and I come back to it again and again. The psalm was possibly written to mark the return of the 'Ark of the Lord' to Jerusalem from the house of Obed-Edom. (2 Samuel 6:12-19). It would have been sung as the procession approached the city gates and since, for the Israelites, the Ark embodied the presence of God there was great celebration on its return.

When I want to wait on the Lord, and to feel my heart entwined with His, and there seems to be too much interference from unhelpful rogue thoughts, I envisage my heart as that city of Jerusalem. I want to focus on the Lord and His presence with me. I want to hear His whispers as I go through the day, but my heart is heavy, and so I need to ask Him to come and deal with the enemy within and restore His peace to my mind and heart. The picture from the psalm that I find most helpful, at this point, is in verse seven, 'Lift up your heads, O you gates; be lifted up, you ancient doors, that the King of glory may come in.' Then follows that wonderful question, 'Who is this King of glory?' and the answering cry, 'The Lord strong and mighty, the Lord mighty in battle.' And again in verse 10 'The Lord Almighty – he is the King of glory'.

If I want the 'King of Glory, the Lord strong and mighty in battle' to help me win the battle in my mind, then I need to invite Him in. I need to lift my head and open up the doors to the citadel that is my heart and welcome Him. Now we know that the Lord lives within by His Spirit so it is not that He is not with me at all, but we also know that the Holy Spirit will come afresh to us as we ask and pray for more of His presence. (Acts 4:29-31).

These verses from Psalm 24 remind me who it is that I am inviting into my heart afresh; the King of Kings 'mighty and powerful in battle'; the one who can deal with the battle in my mind too. So I set about opening up the gates in order to let Him come in, in battle array. The psalm describes this as 'lifting up', and this idea of 'lifting up' is linked with rejoicing, praise and thanksgiving. It is interesting how often our intention is mirrored by our posture and certainly lifting our heads, hands and voices can make a big difference to us spiritually, as we open up afresh to the Lord.

When the Lord comes, those inner battles which are fuelled by the lies of the enemy, are won by the 'truth'. As I worship, the Holy Spirit will speak the truth I need to hear into my heart, mind and spirit. Now we know that Jesus defeated the devil in the wilderness using 'truth', (Matthew 4:1-11), and so can we, as we lift our heads and welcome the King of Glory in to fight with and for us. Then we can again entwine our hearts with His.

Activation . . .

Today let thanksgiving, even for small and everyday things, be the key that flings wide those doors for you, as you let the King of Glory in to fight with you in any battles that are going on. Those doors may feel tightly shut, but thanksgiving is a powerful key and one that we can freely use at anytime, to swing the doors open and welcome into our hearts and minds our strong and mighty King of Glory.

DAY 221 | Thanksgiving and My Perspective

A strange thing happens when I give thanks; I see things very differently. Giants and big mountains become opportunities for a miracle, and irritations become like the grit in an oyster's shell. They become the opportunity to create a pearl. I first learnt that lesson many years ago, but it is of course one that has to be learnt again many times over. It's a recurring theme throughout life that the Holy Spirit will use those things, (and people), that irritate and annoy, to produce something Christ like and beautiful in our lives.

Impatience has always been my big one, waiting around for something to happen has always felt like a waste of time, unproductive time that could be better used in better ways. Giving thanks, rather than getting fretful and frustrated has made a great difference. Turning to the Lord with a thankful heart releases creativity and I very often find that the Holy Spirit will remind me of something I can do, or someone I can pray for, in the time of waiting.

Sometimes it can result in just taking a moment to 'be still' and reflect. It can also lead to remembering something I was supposed to be doing – which is always helpful! It maybe the chance to take the moment to clear something, prepare something, do something I have been putting off. The lesson is simple; being thankful, even for the wait or the delay that threatens to frustrate, releases a peaceful mindset that enables the Holy Spirit to lead and guide. It brings me into line with David's declaration in Psalm 31:14&15. 'But I trust in you, O Lord; I say "You are my God." My times are in your hands...'.

Taking that lesson into the realm of our human relationships, I have discovered that when I am irritated by someone, or something that someone is doing, giving thanks for that person and the situation changes everything. It first of all changes my perspective as I start to realise that quite often the Lord is drawing my attention to the fact that this person needs me to pray for them. It is quite often the case that He will then prompt me to ask a question or make a comment that causes them to share something of importance that is going on for them.

Secondly I begin to see this person, or what they are doing, as a blessing. As I give thanks for them I begin to see the challenge they present to my peace as the 'grit' in the oyster of my heart that is going to produce a pearl. As I let the Holy Spirit lead and help me, I begin to see what the Lord is endeavoring to change in me. My attitude can then shifts from 'this is a nuisance', to 'OK Lord what is it that you are seeking to refine in me to make me more like Jesus'.

Change can then come in my behavior towards that person or that situation, as the Holy Spirit gives the grace and wisdom to see what He sees and what He would want me to do and say. This will be very different to just 'putting up with something', gritted teeth style, or covering up more unpleasant emotions with a sweet 'Christian' smile.

Father, Son and Holy Spirit will be smiling and enjoying the opportunity to change me first of all, and then bring change in someone else's life or circumstances, using me as a catalyst. Basically I am saying that the Lord 'never misses a trick'. He never misses an opportunity to bless us, do us good and to work in our lives to change us, as well as working through us, and with us, to help others to become more like Him too.

Activation...

Let today be the day when being thankful for irritations opens up a whole new level of walking with Him, where even 'the bits of grit' in your life become fun as you say, "And what are you seeking to change in me today Lord?" and "No I didn't see that one coming, but thank you!"

DAY 222 | Thanksgiving that God doesn't Change

Yesterday we were thinking about how our thanksgiving can change how we see people and situations and also how we behave towards people. Today we are giving thanks for the good news that our God, by contrast, is **unchanging**.

I think we all – well most of us – love a certain amount of familiarity in our lives. Even if we aren't great 'routine' people we still like to live with a fair number of certainties, like the fact that our shops will be well stocked, that our journeys will be a predictable length, or that our income will be steady over a period of time. We can get quite irritated if we are unpredictably let down in these various everyday areas of life, and really big disruptions and changes in life can cause great distress and upset.

The comfortableness of our lives is based on a certain amount of 'knowing what to expect' in a wide variety of situations, and this is why we are 'shaken up' when things go wrong, when things that we have taken for granted are suddenly not behaving in the way that we think they should. Really big changes like the sudden loss of a job, the death of someone close or an unexpected illness, or even the more minor disruptions, like those unexpected road diversions that happen on a journey home late at night, can all unsettle us to varying degrees.

I think for many people big changes and disruptions to the 'predictable' in life cause them to dig deeper into their life with the Lord, and this is good. In all change, big and small, the Lord wants us to know that He is our unshakeable 'Rock'. He is the solid foundation on which we have built our lives. 'Jesus Christ is the same yesterday and today and forever.' (Hebrews 13:8), and if, as He says, everything one day will be shaken that can be shaken, (Hebrews 12:26,2, quoted from Haggai 2:6), then we need to know, very deep down at the core of our being, that we have an unshakable relationship with our unchanging God, and that He will take us through.

The writer of Psalm 46 knew all about this. He writes, 'God is our refuge and strength, an ever present help in trouble. Therefore we will not fear, though the earth give way and the mountains fall into the heart of the sea,' He then describes God's faithfulness to 'the city of God' – that's us His people – saying 'Nations are in uproar, kingdoms fall; He lifts his voice, the earth melts. **The Lord God Almighty is with us; the God of Jacob is our fortress.'** (verses 6&7)

In times of trouble, in times of upheaval in our lives, big and small, that is our confidence, and the psalmist gives us a hint as to how we reach that place of confidence, he speaks to us prophetically, as from the mouth of God, with the words, "Be still, and know that I am God; I will be exalted among the nations, I will be exalted in the earth." The psalmist then makes his own triumphant declaration, "The Lord Almighty is with us; the God of Jacob is our fortress." (verses 10 & 11).

The key, it would seem, to coping with the changeableness of life and the insecurity that that can engender, is simply this: Be still and remember who the 'I Am' is, and who He wants to be for you in each situation. Stop and remind yourself of His names, of who He says that He is and then as you say 'Thank you Lord, You are Jehovah Jireh, my provider; thank you Lord that you are my strength and stay; that you are my rock and fortress; thank you Lord that you are the faithful one' etc. etc., your faith will rise and unexpected changes will no longer hold the terror they once did.

Activation...

Thank God for those unexpected disruptions and changes that come into your life, because they can strengthen you for the 'big ones'. Remember that David learnt to trust the Lord for the bear and the lion, and so had confidence when fighting Goliath, (1 Samuel 17:34-37). Use thanksgiving in the smaller interruptions to the flow of life to build your confidence in your unchanging, faithful God. See how He delivers you in the smaller things, and so find the peace that comes from knowing that He is with you when the bigger challenges in life come along.

'Those who trust in the Lord are like Mount Zion, which cannot be shaken but endures forever. As the mountains surround Jerusalem, so the Lord surrounds His people both now and forevermore.' (Psalm 125:1,2).

DAY 223 | Thanksgiving that we have a Mighty God with a Father's Heart

We have an extraordinary faith. We have an All Mighty God who is the designer and creator of everything, of mind blowing things, of both cosmic and nano size. He is powerful, omnipotent, omniscient, omnipresent, and yet I can say, "This is my Heavenly Father, my good, good Father, and I am His beloved child." These thoughts are so staggering, that we do indeed need the Holy Spirit to help us to grasp them in our minds, hearts and spirits. It is all so far beyond rational thought and belief. (Ephesians 1:17-21, and 3:16-19).

In many ways, we in the western church have been like sleeping beauty; asleep to the immensity of our salvation, and the truth that we are now in this incomparable relationship with the most wonderful being we could ever, ever, ever imagine. We have been asleep to these wonderful realities for a very long time, awaiting our Prince – the Holy Spirit – to come and wake us up. I wonder if that is why previous revivals have been called 'Awakenings', because that is what revival is. It is when these incredible truths become so real to us that we just can't keep our mouths shut, and those outside the church become hungry for what we have.

So how can we possibly know and grasp the reality of who our loving heavenly Father really is, or understand what He is like when our minds are so finite and small. Well, when Philip said to Jesus, "Lord, show us the Father and that will be enough for us." Jesus answered, "Don't you know me, Philip, even after I have been among you such a long time? Anyone who has seen me has seen the Father . . . Believe me when I say that I am in the Father and the Father is in me; or at least believe on the evidence of the miracles themselves." (John 14:8, 9, 11).

So as we look at Jesus we see the miraculous and mighty power that He exercised over the elements, the demons, physical sickness and death itself. We also see and how He was with people, we see the Father in His kindness and compassion, His wisdom and love too. As I read the gospels, the accounts of how Jesus was with people, how He dealt with people from all different walks of life, and the things He taught them – which cut across many of the traditions and practices of the time – I have a lens through which I can see how He would speak to me and how He would show me His love.

There is such a variety of people and situations in the gospels, and the Holy Spirit can use to them to speak into our hearts, highlighting whatever aspect of the Father's heart that we need to hear. This is because, 'He is the image of the invisible God, the firstborn over all creation. For by him all things were created; things in heaven and on earth, visible and invisible ... all things were created by him and for him.' 'For God was pleased to have **all His fullness dwell in him**.' (Colossians 1:15,16 & 19). We also read from another New Testament letter writer that, 'The Son is the radiance of God's Glory and the exact representation of His being, sustaining all things by his powerful word.' (Hebrews 1:3).

Activation...

Make today a day of thanksgiving that our Heavenly Father gave us, not just a Saviour in Jesus, but a template of who He Himself is. He gave us a visual aid in Jesus; one that we could understand with our earthbound minds and hearts. Thank Him that those stories of Jesus were written down for us, and so value them again as a window into the heart of the Almighty One.

Then thank the Father for sending the precious Holy Spirit who will lead you into all truth, (John 14:16, 17 & 26). Thank Him that He will show you those aspects of the Father in the life of Jesus that you need to know in your life today. Give thanks to the Father also because He is sending the Holy Spirit to 'wake us up' to some fresh and wonderful truths, as we look again and again at the things recorded.

I believe that as we approach all these things again with hearts filled with gratitude we will see wonderful things about our God and about our place in His heart. We will see things that, till now, we have not properly grasped, becoming ever more real to us. Give thanks and let your heart be filled with joy as today you 'draw more water from the wells of salvation.' (Isaiah 12:3).

DAY 224 | Thanksgiving and Holiness

The bible has a lot to say about Holiness. We read a lot about the holiness of God in the Old Testament in the books of Moses, in Isaiah's call to ministry, (Isaiah 6) and in the Psalms (e.g. Psalm 99:3, 5, & 9). Incredibly we discover in the New Testament that, as believers, God sees us as holy and dearly loved, (Colossians 3:12), and He wants us to be holy in our lives as He is holy 'Just as he who called you is holy, so be holy in all you do; for it is written: "Be holy, because I am holy." (1 Peter 1:15, 16).

As a young Christian, I found the topic of the 'Holiness of God' somewhat scary and the call to be holy was accompanied by a significant fear of failing. This resulted in a mixture of feeling pressured to be something I was not, along with an anxiety that I was falling short. The truth is God is perfect and perfectly holy, awesomely so, and clearly no one can approach him in their own righteousness. Alongside that reality there is the truth that we are not perfect. However we can now stand before God fully righteous in Jesus' righteousness, at the same time as we are being changed, step by step, to be more like Him; being conformed to the image of His Son (Romans 8:29). Now there is something to get excited about and to be very thankful for!

Today we can reflect on another aspect of holiness that I believe is wonderful and life changing and which can grow and thrill me, fuelled by thanksgiving. Holy means separate or set apart, Holiness is separation. A place, thing, (or person) set apart. Now what about that romantic novel "He/she only had eyes for his/her beloved"? This is very exciting. When you are deeply in love with someone, you don't go out with someone else primarily because there are rules saying you shouldn't. No! You don't go out with others because you are deeply in love with one person. You are set apart, or separated from others because of the love you have for 'the one'.

So does thanksgiving really play a part here? Well it works in the human realm. The more grateful and thankful I am for my partner and his/her qualities – personal, emotional, practical, physical, intellectual, skillful, spiritual and more – the more I grow in appreciation of them. Then I become even more thankful, and as I do the more beautiful, in all aspects, they become to me and the more set apart, separate, or holy the relationship will be. Now this doesn't work just for your life partner, the same principle of noticing and being thankful works with your friends, your children, your church leader etc, etc; gratitude and thanksgiving increases appreciation.

And I want to suggest that this is so with God too. Thanksgiving, fueled by noticing all that God is, what it means to belong to His family and be 'His Beloved'; noticing all that He has done, is doing and promises He will do for me, stokes up my love for Him. And love increasingly only has eyes for its beloved. And there it is, set apart holiness on the increase. Not duty and falling short but increasingly intoxicated by love. David lived a lot in thanksgiving and praise and had a brilliantly close relationship with the Lord.

Now you may say I am being idealistic. No, this is a journey. Anyone who has been in love knows there are ups and downs in life as well as in the novels. We may have eyes for others (or other things), and go off course in one way or another, even hurt each other. David did, but grace, love and forgiveness brought him back into relationship. And it is also true that genuine, full blown love does involve work, perseverance and sacrifice. So it is with the pursuit of our Holy Lord.

Activation...

Ask the Holy Spirit if there is more to the pursuit of holiness and our Holy God than you have seen so far, and ask whether it might be more of a huge romance than you had previously thought. Pull that weapon of thanksgiving out again, the one that you have been practicing over the last few months. See if it isn't powerful in further fueling your love and appreciation for your beloved Lord as you notice and appreciate Him more and more. As you remind yourself in thanksgiving of all He is and has done and is doing for you. And as you notice and appreciate how beloved you are to Him, it could result in a whole new perspective on being holy and set apart for Him than you have previously had.

DAY 225 | Thanksgiving, Love and being Holy

Following on from yesterday's meditation on 'Thanksgiving and Holiness' I wanted to share more on the theme of 'Holiness' with some thoughts gleaned from a paper I read very recently by Bob Mumford entitled 'Stepping over the Threshold'. In this paper he shares some really illuminating insights into what he believes is happening, both in the world and the church at this moment in time. In the course of writing about these things he explains the difference between the two Hebrew words for Holy, 'Qodesh' and 'Chaciyd', the second of which is more often written as the word 'Hesed'.

As we pointed out yesterday, 'being holy' and 'being set apart', are linked to being loved. We wrote, 'When you are deeply in love with someone, you don't go out with someone else because of the rules saying you shouldn't. No! You don't go out with others because you are in love with one person. You are set apart, or separate, because of love for the one you love'.

This was confirmed to me as I read Bob Mumford's explanation of those two Hebrew words[2]. The word 'qodesh', used many times in the Old Testament is often used about God. Our Holy God. A God like no other, totally set apart and higher than any other being ever. The word 'hesed', used much less in the Old Testament, is applied to 'a holy one', a saint, or a godly one.

Bob Mumford quotes Rev. Willis Judson Beecher saying, 'Hesed denotes a kindly loved one, a **favoured one**, one who is **in favour**, a **favourite one** who is the object of gracious love and is treated accordingly. That is, it denotes a person in whom loving kindness is thought of as resident.'[1] It is no wonder then that Paul could write instruction to the early Christians, starting with a reminder of their standing with God. He writes, 'Therefore as God's chosen people, **holy and dearly loved,** clothe yourselves with compassion, kindness, humility, gentleness and patience.' (Colossians 3:12). (All bold emphasis here is mine.)

So there it is! We are all God's favourites. I knew it!!! We are His holy ones and the recipients of His gracious love and undeserved favour. At this point we need to put aside our modern understanding of favourite, because in our world a person can only have one favourite; the problem then is that often, that one person is spoilt, or gets away with too much. They then provoke envy and jealousy from others who don't feel so special.

Looking up the meaning of the suffix –ite, I read, 'it is a suffix, of Greek origin, indicating relation to the thing signified by the noun to which it is attached'. Simply put, by way of an example, an Israelite is one who is attached to Israel. So if you and I are God's 'favour – ite', it means that we are 'attached' to God's favour, which is boundless towards each one of us. How wonderful is that? And He won't spoil us, because as part of that favour He will discipline us with love. (Something which we will be considering on Day 231.)

Activation . . .

Today however let us personalise this wonderful truth. We can thank Him that we are His chosen and set apart ones. We are His 'hesed' ones, His favour-ites. I think that as we do this we will appreciate more and more what amazing favour we are in fact living under, and that in turn will cause us to long to please Him in all that we do. We will be His set apart ones, because we will have eyes for no other. We will grow, and increasingly become the beautiful bride that He has won by His love and sacrifice.

Let all who take refuge in you be glad: let them ever sing for joy. Spread your protection over them, that those who love your name may rejoice in you. For surely, O Lord, you bless the righteous; you surround them with your favour as a shield. (Psalm 5:11,12).

DAY 226 | Thanksgiving for His Complete Acceptance

I think it's true to say that most of us, without doubt, want to feel loved and accepted for who we are; loved and accepted by our parents, by our spouse, by our friends, by our church leaders, those we serve and those we work with. Feeling accepted, helps us to feel validated and 'OK' about ourselves. Some relationships don't matter so much and but few people can genuinely say, "I don't care what anyone thinks of me". Even these people, who would say that the opinion of others doesn't count for a great deal, probably know that the opinion of those on whom they feel dependent, like an employer or someone who is going to assess them in some way, does matter.

For the vast majority of us however the desire to be accepted, and to feel as if we belong, is of great importance and can affect how we conduct ourselves in many ways. We see it in the gang member, the pupil with their class mates at school, the family member, and the church member. Feeling unaccepted, is a lonely place and not a position in which many of us like to be. One of the difficulties for us as human beings is that we are flawed. We are 'noble but fallen', as CS Lewis would say. Therefore, although we long for acceptance and the feeling of closeness that it brings, it can be the case that, the closer we get to others, the more our weaknesses and failings can be seen, and not many of us want to experience the rejection that that might precipitate.

When we are children we long for affirmation and acceptance from our parents and primary care givers, and of course they see us at our best and our worst. Loving us includes the task of disciplining and training us, as well as caring, protecting and providing for us. Even if that discipline is administered fairly and correctly we can still grow up feeling that there are things about us that are not acceptable. These feelings can then be reinforced by teachers, and other adults in our lives, who bring also bring correction.

If that is so we sometimes learn to hide, to keep our distance from people. We learn to make sure that people see our acceptable face, and maybe we find it hard when some part of us, that we are not so keen about, gets exposed. Some of us work hard to 'please' others, living to gain approval, but then that in itself does not give us a secure relaxed place in life because there is always the risk of being 'found out' if people really get to know us.

Well the amazing thing about our wonderful heavenly Father is that He knows us completely and utterly, even better than we know ourselves, (Psalm 139:1-6), and yet we are totally 'accepted in the beloved', (Ephesians 1:6 AV). The Passion Translation puts that very mystical passage in these words, 'Because of His great love, He ordained us, so that we would be seen as holy in His eyes with an unstained innocence. For it was always in His perfect plan to adopt us as His delightful children, through our union with Jesus, the anointed one, **so that His tremendous love that cascades over us would glorify His grace – for the same love He has for His beloved one, Jesus, He has for us.**'

It's not a case of 'love is blind' with God, nor is my acceptance with Him based on my performance, but it is because I am now united with Christ. My heavenly Father can see the problem that I am, and the problems that I have; He can discipline and train me, use every circumstance to make me more like Jesus, and still accept and love me totally and completely as He loves Jesus. Quite amazing!!

If holiness, as we wrote yesterday, is being set apart and special, and we are 'God's chosen people, holy and dearly loved ...' (Colossians 3:12), then we can revel in His acceptance of us. We have no need to 'hide', we are in a relationship where He knows everything about us, and loves us still with a relentless and undying love. Giving thanks for this wonderful truth, helps me to absorb it deep into my being. The acceptance for which I long will then become more and more real in my experience.

Activation ...

Today as you give thanks to God for the wonderful truth of His total acceptance of, and love for you, let the understanding of the depth of the Lord's love for you help you in your acceptance of yourself, and of others.

DAY 227 | Thanksgiving that I now Belong

Just as we can expend much energy in life looking for acceptance, so we can also wander through life feeling that we don't quite belong, and then a similar search can go on as I look for somewhere to belong, somewhere I can 'put my feet up'. So let's have a look at one of the wonderful side effects of knowing that I am completely accepted by the Lord – the truth that I now also belong.

I have been adopted into His family and I have a wonderful Heavenly Father. This gives me royal status, I am now a child of the King. Paul writes in Romans 8:15-17. 'For you have not received a spirit of slavery leading to fear again, but you have received a spirit of adoption as sons by which we cry out, "Abba! Father!" The Spirit Himself testifies with our spirit that we are children of God, and if children, heirs also...' (NASB).

When we become Christians it's like finding 'home' for our souls. God wants us to be that sure and that comfortable in His love and acceptance that we can begin to relax in who He has made us to be, even if the world around us makes us feel that we don't quite fit the mould! Furthermore not only do I belong in God's family, but the wonderful thing about being adopted is that the adopter knew what they were getting and still chose to go ahead with the adoption. Part of being totally accepted by God is the knowledge that He wanted me in His family, even before He had begun to work on my transformation.

This is just so important, because if I can believe that I am accepted and that I belong in God's family, not because I snuck in the back door when He wasn't looking, but because He chose to adopt me into His family, I can accept myself at a much deeper level. I no longer need to try to be like someone else who I admire, or try to be the person that I think others want me to be. To be accepted and belong I don't even need to be the sort of person I imagine God would want me to be, because I am mistakenly thinking that His acceptance is conditional. I can come 'Just as I am'!

The bottom line is that it means I can stop comparing myself – such a big problem in our social media generation – in terms of looks, achievement, income, occupation, friendships etc. etc. I once heard a wise comment about the fact that it is a waste of time wanting to be like someone else because that position is already taken! A little glib perhaps, but it is the negative side of another definition I heard about having a healthy amount of self esteem. It was simply this: A good sense of self esteem manifests itself as 'the joy of being me'.

There's an expression we use sometimes, "I'm going to make the most of this". It has the slight overtones of 'making the best of a bad job', but someone I know took that phrase, 'make the most', as a motto and found that it transformed the way she saw life – for the better – and in a very tangible way. The fact is there is only one of me and one of you! That 'you' is totally unique in every aspect of your life, and no one else has the opportunities, the relationships, the qualities, the life experience that you have. If you and I can believe that and embrace who we are because we have been embraced by, and belong to, the great and Mighty King of all the earth, we will 'make the most' of everything He has given us.

When we do that everything becomes more meaningful and rich. And this journey into meaningful belonging will all start with thanking Him for the incredible privilege of belonging to Him, having been adopted into His family because of Jesus death in our place and His resurrection that gives us a new life. God has chosen to have me in His family. I am accepted and I belong to Him. So today let us give ourselves to thanksgiving that we belong to a wonderful heavenly Father. Let that release a deep sense of belonging into the depths of our hearts, with a sense also of our preciousness and our value to Him.

Activation...

Thank the Lord today for this wonderful truth that you totally and utterly belong to Him. The mystery is that when we realise and revel in this truth the Holy Spirit finds it a lot easier to do His transforming work in our lives; and so we become more like Jesus day by day.

DAY 228 | Thanksgiving and Accepting Others

It is so important that in God's family we know that we are accepted and that we belong, and I am not simply talking here about feeling OK when we go into a church. Sadly it can be the case for many to go to church and still feel that they don't belong, or that they are not accepted. I guess this is because in the church we are joining with others who are 'a work in progress' like ourselves; even the leaders. If the church is a community of people who have been saved by grace, then it's no surprise that we are going to encounter a lot of imperfection even in the best of churches.

My sense of acceptance and belonging has to go deeper than how I am treated by other people, hence the previous two days reflections about God's acceptance of me. If I am deeply secure in the Lord's love and acceptance, even though I know there is much about me yet to be changed, then the affirmation and acceptance of others will be a great blessing, but I am less likely to feel rejected if it is not there, or not in evidence for some reason.

More importantly, understanding and taking in the depth of the Lord's love for me will help me in my acceptance of both myself, and then of others. If I find within myself a contentment with who I am, coming from that sense of belonging to the Lord, then I will myself find it easier to accept others. Sadly when I don't feel accepted myself I am more likely to be critical of others and indignant when they appear to be more at ease than me in the community. So let's do a little Bible study and listen in to Paul's admonition to the believers in and around Colossae and note the order of his admonitions.

First of all we hear, acceptance and belonging for ourselves in the words...

'Therefore as God's chosen people, holy and dearly loved,'

Then the encouragement to be nice to others!!!

'clothe yourselves with compassion, kindness, humility, gentleness and patience.'

He carries on with great realism that we all need grace,

'**Bear with each other and forgive whatever grievances you may have against one another. Forgive as the Lord forgave you. And over all these virtues put on love, which binds them all together in perfect unity.**'

He then reminds us that our fellow believers have also been adopted and accepted and they also 'belong'.

'**Let the peace of Christ rule in your hearts, since as members of one body you were called to peace.**'

And what do you think comes next??

'**And be thankful.**'

He then recognises that there will be a need for growth and correction saying ...

'**Let the word of Christ dwell in you richly as you teach and admonish one another with all wisdom,**'

With of course ... more praise and thanksgiving!!

'**and as you sing psalms, hymns and spiritual songs with gratitude in your hearts to God.**'

And a bit more thanksgiving to finish up with ...

'**And whatever you do, whether in word or deed, do it all in the name of Jesus, giving thanks to God the Father through Him.**' (Colossians 3:12-17).

Activation ...

As being thankful helps you yourself to feel loved, accepted and that you belong, let it also help you to accept others as you thank God for His acceptance of them. Then let thanksgiving help you to love others even as you teach and admonish each other positively, should the opportunity arise.

DAY 229 | Thanksgiving For God's Protection

A few days ago we were looking at the wonderful truth that we have been adopted into God's family. That means that I know I have a wonderful Heavenly Father. Perfect in every way! This brings that incredible sense of belonging and acceptance and also many blessings that we can now reckon on, as we travel through life. We don't have to 'keep in with Him' or 'keep Him happy', like a slave, servant, or even as an employee. We are His beloved children and nothing can change that. Even if we walk away from Him for a while, He won't sever the connection, as illustrated for us in the story of the prodigal son. There is such safety in this relationship, such security!

There is also great protection. Now this is a mystery, one that causes a lot of God's children a lot of trouble. We read Psalm 91:9-14, and feel greatly comforted, and then we hear of something very hard happening to one of God's children, or indeed to ourselves, and we get confused. "Was I meant to take those verses literally?" Or "Have I done something wrong?" "What is happening here? Has God forgotten me?"

Well, the promises of God are for us in a fallen world, where all sorts of things are going wrong. The world is under the influence of 'the prince of the power of the air, of the spirit now working in the sons of disobedience.' (Ephesians 2:2. NASB). How else can we explain some of the dark, dark things that go on in God's beautiful world, and the madness we see all around us? The spiritual power of 'the prince of the power of the air' works its way out in our world in all sorts of destructive ways, politically, socially and physically, and of course relationally.

It is in this context that the Lord promises to be with us, to help and protect us. Jesus 'the Prince of Peace' Himself said, "I have told you these things, so that in me you might have peace. In this world you will have trouble. But take heart! I have overcome the world." (John 16:33). The psalmist does understand this paradox, and so writes at the end of Psalm 91 in verses 14 and 15, "Because he loves me," says the Lord, "I will rescue him; I will protect him, for he acknowledges my name. He will call upon me, and I will answer him; I will be with Him in trouble, I will deliver and honour him, and show him my salvation."

Basically we wouldn't need the protection of our heavenly Father if we lived in a perfect world where there was no trouble, or if He just cocooned us all, until He took us up to heaven. For us it is neither of those scenarios. There is trouble all around us, and God does not always helicopter us out of it, but walks through it with us. It is because of His presence – because the Almighty is with us – that we are protected.

Paul so understood this, and spells it out for us in Romans 8:35-39, 'Who shall separate us from the love of Christ? Shall trouble or hardship or persecution or famine or nakedness or danger or sword? ... No **in all these things** we are more than conquerors through Him who loved us. For I am convinced that neither death nor life, neither angels nor demons, neither the present nor the future, nor any powers, neither height nor depth, nor anything else in all creation, will be able to separate us from the love of God that is in Christ Jesus our Lord.'

Sometimes that protection is obvious. We are literally stopped from falling under a bus, so to speak. Sometimes trouble hits us, (No pun meant!!), and we have to call on the Lord for our deliverances. Sometimes those deliverances come in this life, sometimes not. I think of Corrie Ten Boom and her sister Betsy. Betsy died in the concentration camp; Corrie was miraculously released for some unknown reason, shortly before the war ended. They both loved the Lord. Was one more protected than the other? I think not. Corrie found great peace when she saw the body of her beloved Betsy though the window and saw that she died with a smile on her face. The Lord had come for her, all suffering ended. Corrie on the other hand still had work to do here on earth, and was set free to do it.

Activation...

Thanksgiving will enable you to receive the Lords provision and help in whatever way He chooses to give it to you. Let it be a guard protecting your mind from feeling that the Lord's deliverance will come in a certain way.

DAY 230 | Thanksgiving For God's Provision

Another wonderful blessing which comes from having our God as our heavenly Father is that He not only promises to be my protector, but I can be absolutely certain He, 'my provider', is never short of anything that I need. That in itself is worth at least a day's thanksgiving!!! Now the name of God, Jehovah-Jireh, that we quote when thinking about God's provision for us, was of course given to Abraham at a point in His life when he was going to demonstrate his faith in God by literally, physically sacrificing his only son, his son of promise. God steps in and 'provides' a ram for the sacrifice, so that Isaac is spared, and Abraham calls that place, 'The Lord Will Provide'. The scripture then continues with the words, 'On the mountain of the Lord it will be provided.' (Genesis 22:12-14).

It seems to me that this indicates that God will provide all that I need to serve Him, or all that I need as His child to honour Him, as I live in obedience and submission to Him. It is not about Him giving us free handouts to satisfy our every whim, particularly if we are living independent lives outside of His will for us. Nor does He give us excessive amounts of provision to bank, like a win on the lottery so that we could say once and for all 'I am provided for'. God's provision comes in the context of our relationship with Him and is an ongoing daily experience for us, keeping us close to His heart.

We see this in the story Jesus told about the prodigal son written down for us in Luke 15:11-32. When the son was given his inheritance in one lump sum, he left his father house, went astray, and lost it all. Although he is in need, the Father does not go running to him with more funds! And so in the middle section of the story the son experiences unmet need, the father is no longer 'providing' for him. However when he comes back into relationship with the father through remorse and repentance – when relationship is restored – then the father again blesses and provides for him with a great celebration.

Another verse that we love to quote is Psalm 23:1, 'The Lord is my shepherd I shall not want...' This is then followed by all the wonderful ways in which the Lord, our Shepherd, does indeed provide and look after us. I think that sometimes we miss the powerful declaration that is made at the beginning of this psalm, which could in fact be written with the added words, *'Because I have made* the Lord my shepherd, I shall not want'. There is here the implication that I am surrendered to the Lordship of Christ. That He leads where He wants me to go and **the provision follows me because I follow Him.**

The point I am making is this. There is no shortage of resource available to me in Christ. Father God is indeed my provider because I am 'in Christ' and Christ is in me. Everything that I need is indeed already now mine. It is part of my inheritance. It is paid for because I am now 'in Christ' and I now stand before God as a joint heir with Him, and 'how will He not also with Him freely give us all things?' (Romans 8:32, NASB). Moreover unlike our gas and electricity charges, the tariff is not going to change, it has all been prepaid, and not by us. I can be full of thanks for these truths, but in order to be in a place where I am continually aware of, and receiving, God's provision, I need to stand near to Him, and walk closely with Him day by day.

Giving thanks for these amazing truths enables me to receive the blessings and live day by day enjoying the benefits of all that Christ has won for me, but I will never manage to do that in my own strength, or ever be good enough to deserve this kind of favour. It is all received by faith. Staying in a place of thanksgiving as a child with my Heavenly Father, enables me to do just that, to stay in faith. Gratitude keeps me close to His heart, enabling me to see the smile on His face as He gladly releases all that I need moment by moment as we walk through life together. I can then confidently say, "This is **my** Shepherd, **my** Jehovah-Jireh."

Activation...

I leave you today with some verses to ponder from Romans 8:16,17, from The Passion Translation.

'For the Holy Spirit makes God's fatherhood real to us as He whispers into our innermost being, "You are God's beloved child!" And since we are His true children, we qualify to share all His treasures, for indeed, we are heirs of God Himself. And since we are joined to Christ, we also inherit all that He is and all that He has. We will experience being co-glorified with Him provided that we accept his sufferings as our own.'

DAY 231 | Thanksgiving For God's Dicipline

Discipline often gets quite a bad press with, perhaps, a grudging acknowledgement that it is a 'necessary evil' in life. In order to teach a classroom full of children a teacher, for example, needs to have 'good discipline'. Being known as 'a disciplinarian', however, is not always a compliment. It can have broad associations with not just staying in control but of being 'controlling' which carries with it the notion that negative emotions, like guilt and fear, will be used to achieve the goal and keep people 'in line' – itself a military concept. How different then from the heart of our Heavenly Father who 'disciplines those he loves,' (Hebrews 12:6).

Somehow in our warped world, discipline and love have been separated. Teaching a child, "no you can't do that." has somehow become a negative that shouldn't be part of the parenting vocabulary. The love and kindness involved in setting good boundaries has been confused with being controlling, and so, often, children can grow up all at sea, unable to understand why they are not allowed all the freedom they want even if it is at their own, or someone else's, expense.

True discipline, (the word coming from the same root as disciple), is about learning, growing and maturing. And so if we are Jesus' disciples then we can reckon that the Almighty, who is also our loving Heavenly Father, will be bringing some discipline into our lives. The point is that even though we are totally accepted by Him, and adopted into His family by grace, (see Days 225,226,228) He loves us too much to leave us as we are.

Our Heavenly Father has purposed that we will be changed into Jesus' likeness and Jesus is ever living to intercede for us on this journey, (Hebrews 7:25), and the Holy Spirit is constantly working in our lives to help, teach, train and guide us. 'The Three' will work through every possible means until Christ is formed in us. Now being disciplined by God is not like being sent to the headmaster's office. It is rather part of walking with the Trinity and accepting their wisdom, training and correction as we go, just as the disciples did with Jesus.

Quite often when the disciples had overstepped the mark and got it wrong in some way, Jesus just sat them down, or took them aside, and taught them a better way. We can read a beautiful example of this in Luke 9:46-55. Jesus was constantly correcting and training them as they walked with Him daily, and He will do the same for us. Sometimes it's about taking those moments and turning to Him with honesty in our hearts saying, "I didn't do that very well Lord, how could I have done that differently?"

If that sounds a little too idealistic, (and I don't think any of us really like having our faults and failings pointed out to us) then the writer to the Hebrews paints a more realistic picture about how difficult it can be to receive discipline or correction. He writes, 'No discipline seems pleasant at the time, but painful', but he adds, 'Later on however, it produces a harvest of righteousness and peace for those who have been trained by it.' (Hebrews 12:11). Now this passage was written to the Hebrew Christians who were having a hard time and so he is encouraging them to let God use those hardships in order to discipline, train and change them.

We all know that when life is hard some of our weaknesses surface quite uncomfortably, and they can go on display for all to see. It's at those times that, James suggests, we should consider these trials as 'pure joy', (James 1:2) because God is going to work some very good things into our character through them. And so staying in an attitude of gratefulness for His correction does just that and it also keeps us open and sensitive to His prompting and leading. It should be noted at this point, that God does not always have to use hardship to teach us. There is the joy of reading God's word and letting it 'train us', see 2 Timothy 3:16. There is the joy of letting the Holy Spirit speak to us about our attitudes and better ways to handle different situations, and then there is the fellowship of our brothers and sisters, if we let them close enough, so that iron sharpens iron. (Proverbs 27:17).

Activation . . .

We can just be so thankful that we have a good and wise Heavenly Father who disciplines us out of His great love. So determine today to keep your heart in thankfulness that God **always** disciplines us for our good, then I believe you will find that 'being corrected' will become a source of joy and even hope.

DAY 232 | Thanksgiving for Choice

When we talk about the Lord's disciplining of us, His children, it is important that we see that He never uses coercion. The Lord never seeks to control us like robots. We said yesterday that there are times when God uses hardship to discipline us. He can also use difficulties and trouble to cause us to turn back to Him when we have wandered off course, as He did for the nation of Israel time and time again, when they forgot Him, or went after other gods. But always the choice whether or not to turn back to Him was – and is now for us – given.

Choice is one of the most precious gifts that our Father God gave mankind, but it is one that cost Him greatly. It meant that His precious son Jesus would go to the cross and pay the price for all our bad choices. Freedom to choose, clearly played a significant part when Adam and Eve were tempted and turned away from God in the Garden. And if the devil can't manipulate us into make bad choices, like they did, 'choice' is something that he will seek to destroy and take away from humanity.

He does this in many ways, both on the world stage through political forces and oppression, and in individual lives through fear, through addictions, and through making people into victims of their own or other people's choices. This is why, as a significant part of His 'mission statement' Jesus declared that "The Spirit of the Lord is upon me, because he has anointed me to preach good news to the poor. He has sent me to proclaim freedom for the prisoners and recovery of sight for the blind, to release the oppressed, to proclaim the year of the Lord's favour." (Luke 4:18,19).

We see Jesus demonstrate this freedom, when He lets the rich young man walk away even tho' He loved him. (Mark 10:17-22). Jesus never threatened or even cajoled, He always invited people saying, "Follow Me", as He walked by, (Luke 5:27). We can see too how, giving mankind this freedom to choose, cost Him greatly as He wept over Jerusalem at their refusal to come to Him. (Luke 19:41, and Matthew 23:37). Even when Judas made his decision to betray Jesus, there was no attempt to control. Jesus warned him of the consequences, but made no attempt to dissuade or stop him. (Mark 14:20).

It is important for us to know that Jesus didn't set us free from 'the law of sin and death' (Romans 8:2), or from slavery to sin, to bring us into a controlling relationship. He set us free to restore to us the dignity, given at the creation of mankind; the dignity of having the choice whether or not to follow Him, listen to Him, serve and obey Him.

In making Him the Lord of our lives, as well as our Saviour, we are not surrendering our ability to choose but we are saying, "Lord I want to live every moment in accordance with your will for my life". And because I know that His plans for me are good, that He loves me completely, and that He knows far better than I do what is best for me, I want to make those choices that are in accordance with His will for me. This is Biblical 'surrender'

So how does this all now work for us, His beloved children? We have chosen to 'follow Him', we have 'given our lives to Him', and whatever expression we use to describe the decision we have made, we are now His children. He is committed to discipling us, training us and 'growing us up' and making us more like Jesus, but this never means that He 'controls' us. We still have our freewill, and we are always able to make our choices, but He will always be there, and loves to guide and lead us.

Every day we are faced with myriads of choices, big and small, and staying in a place of thankfulness, that the Lord is with me, that He loves me and wants me to make the best choices, keeps me in good relationship with Him. It also keeps my ear attentive to His promptings and checks.

Activation ...

Take the time today to be thankful for this wonderful gift of 'choice', and take the moment to give thanks, particularly when you are faced with a difficult decision. This will help you to 'pause a moment', thereby allowing your spirit to partner with Holy Spirit, so that your spirit takes the lead over your thoughts and emotions. Then you will be able to say, like David, with confidence and certainty, "He guides me in paths of righteousness for His names sake". (Psalm 23:3).

DAY 233 | Thanksgiving and My Choices

The wonderful gift that God has given mankind called 'freedom to choose', about which we were sharing yesterday, forms an amazing and vital part in our relationship with the Almighty God, our loving Heavenly Father. It can, however, cause us some anxiety particularly if we see following Jesus as a bit of a tightrope. By that I mean that we can feel that it is a very narrow, small, tight path, and that should we veer to left or right we will inevitably fall and have great difficulty getting back on track again.

If we see our life with Jesus like that it's all a bit binary and so I could go wrong at any moment. Every choice is vital because I am either going to make the right choice or the wrong one. This idea that in each situation there is a risk of making the wrong decision can come from our own or other peoples perfectionist perception of life, or even from a wrong understanding of Jesus' words that "... small is the gate and narrow is the road that leads to life, and only a few find it." (Matthew 7:14).

Those words of Jesus refer, I believe, to that choice that we have to follow Jesus, to commit our whole life into His hands. He describes Himself as 'the door' or gate, and any doorway is essentially a narrow place in or out of somewhere. Once through the doorway however we usually come into a very broad, even spacious place. This is because a door is an entrance, (or exit) from one place to another. Jesus, through His cross and resurrection, is our 'narrow' doorway to eternal life, (John 14:6), which is then a wonderfully broad and endless experience of life in all its fullness. (John 10:9,10).

Once we are in the Kingdom of God, having left the kingdom of darkness through Jesus the narrow 'door', we find ourselves in that spiritually broad and spacious place. And in contrast to the tightrope metaphor, the wonderful thing about the Christian life that it is about walking **with** Jesus, not getting it all right 'for' Him. In addition we have the indwelling Holy Spirit to help us as we walk with Him and so the Christian life is not primarily about right and wrong decisions, it's all about relationship, not rules. God doesn't just give us the map, waiting to reprimand us if we make a wrong turn, He comes with us as our guide and helper.

Sometimes we may feel that we really don't know which way to take. Then again we can rely on God's own promises. We can make our choices, trusting that He will help us should we be heading in the wrong direction. He promised the children of Israel, and us too, 'Whether you turn to the right or to the left, your ears will hear a voice behind you, saying "This is the way; walk in it"'. (Isaiah 30:21). In other words He will give us some course correction as we are moving forward, as He did for Paul. (Acts 16:6-10)

So what if I do make a wrong choice, or several wrong choices, choosing to go against some clear instruction in scripture, the promptings of the Holy Spirit or even my own common sense? Well, we have many instances of the Lord graciously redeeming the situation from the lives of the disciples, and I am sure from our own lives. He is SO gracious and longsuffering with us and He somehow manages to weave all our mistakes into a beautiful pattern. He WILL use everything to conform us to His image, (Romans 8:28,29), even the deviations and diversions along the way that we sometimes foolishly insist on taking. I am always greatly comforted at these times by some verses David wrote in one of his psalms.

*As for God, his way is perfect; the word of the Lord is flawless. He is a shield for all who take refuge in him. For who is God besides the Lord? And who is a Rock except our God? It is God who arms me with strength **and makes my way perfect.**'* (Psalm 18:30-32).

Activation ...

Once again staying in an attitude of thankfulness is a big key. As I thank the Lord that He is with me and that the Holy Spirit is my friend and helper, my 'alongsider' in all the decisions, big and small, that I have to make daily, I will find His life flowing through me enabling me to walk freely. Stay in thanksgiving and relish and enjoy making your choices, knowing that it is a precious gift and a wonderful part of growing in your relationship with our loving Shepherd, Jesus.

DAY 234 | Thanksgiving and Solving Problems

Another wonderful thing about being a child of God is that our incredibly kind Heavenly Father helps us to 'in all things to grow up into him who is the Head, that is, Christ.' (Ephesians 4:15). One of the ways in which He does this is by helping us with, and guiding us through, our problems. And yes! Don't be surprised or put out by them, we do all have problems – it's part of being human and alive. When we are children, we look to our parents to solve all our problems, and as parents of small children, we gladly take on that role. As our children grow up, however, I think that as good parents we take a more supportive role, helping our children to develop problem solving skills for themselves. Letting them solve their own problems is never easy and in fact can be very messy, but it's a really important part of 'letting go' and letting them grow up. God I think does something similar.

We had a wonderful friend, who had a little mantra he frequently shared with us. He would say "No problems? No progress!" It never failed to raise a smile and lift our mood, and more recently we have heard Graham Cooke's take on this idea, with his pretend phone call with his friend. Talking to this friend, he commiserates with him that he (the friend) doesn't currently have any problems. He shares how excited he himself is that he now has a big one to deal with. He will pray, he says for this friend, that the Lord would bless him and send him something of a problem soon!!! How's that for faith in our wonderful heavenly Father's love and care for us?

We were looking yesterday at the fact that God gives us the gift of choice, and we can see how important that is in our need to solve the problems that come our way while we are living here on earth. As a good Father, He doesn't magic us out of our problems, or make the problems disappear, but He does always offer His help and support. God is the Great Creator, nothing is too difficult for Him and we, being made in His image, have the ability to be creative and to problem solve too. Like a good parent He 'believes' in us to find creative solutions with the help of our friend, counsellor, and source of power, the Holy Spirit.

Arthur Burke writes in his book, 'Blessing your Spirit'[1], 'There is a time and place for God to lift you out of a tight spot, to rescue you ... A time and place for Him to give you favour in the eyes of people who should be your enemies. But there is a greater joy than either of those – that is the joy of discovering God's wisdom that flows in solving problems.' He refers to 'the manifold wisdom of God', from Ephesians 3:10, that is now to be displayed through the church. The Greek word translated manifold here, actually means 'many coloured'. I like that! For any difficult situation in which I find myself, there is a 'many coloured' wisdom for me in Christ, and I can draw on that wisdom with the Holy Spirit's help. This will bring glory to God as His wisdom flows through my life as I solve, or navigate my way through my problems. The Holy Spirit will help me to 'think outside the box', as I apply this Godly wisdom to a whole variety of situations.

We see this being manifested in both Old and New Testament. In the Old Testament very unconventional methods are used to win wars. Have a look, for example, at Gideon's God given strategy in Judges Chapter 7. While in the New Testament we see Jesus, time and time again, handling difficult people and situations with the utmost wisdom and ease. Read Mark 12:13-34, and watch Jesus handling His enemies trick questions. It's just brilliant!

Today we can be so, so grateful that we have a wonderful heavenly Father who gives us the privilege of 'growing up into Christ in all things'. We can therefore 'give thanks' for **every** problem that we have. That's right, **every** problem!! Graham Cooke's encouragement (after the phone call to his friend) is that with every **problem** there is a **promise** and **provision**. So we can be grateful that there is always the promise of wisdom if we ask for it from God, 'who gives generously to all without finding fault.' (James 1:5).

Activation ...

Today ask with faith expressed by your thanksgiving, for that wisdom, the 'pure, peaceable, gentle, reasonable, full of mercy and good fruits,' wisdom from above, (James 3:17, NASB), Let that wisdom that is very different to the world's wisdom flow into you, bringing glory to God as it helps you to solve your problems and to shine as His child in a dark world.

DAY 235 | Thanksgiving and True Love

It seems to me that the word 'love' and the ideas behind it have changed quite significantly over recent years. People still like to read 1 Corinthians 13 about love at a wedding, but the modern use of the word love frequently has quite a different emphasis. It can even be quite trivial. We talk, for example, about loving chocolate ice cream, loving my new car or my new phone and much more, when we mean that we like them very much. In the New Testament, however, **love always has the good of another person** at its core. By contrast in the examples above you, or I, are at the centre and the chocolate, car or new phone are making us feel good.

This might be a trivial point if the same thing didn't often apply to how society, and perhaps we ourselves see love for other people in these days. The weight of I Corinthians 13 in a marriage service, however, is that I am in this relationship to put you first. Of course I am thrilled to be with you, and to be with you means the world to me, and I am so fortunate to be loved by you. I am therefore receiving a great deal, but in response I want to put you first, (with God's help – if I have any sense!), in order to see you blessed and blossoming in the whole of your life.

It is very interesting therefore that Ephesians 5:33 speaks to men and women separately about how they should relate to each other and what love looks like. Significantly it does NOT say what they can demand from the other. It doesn't say a husband should demand his wife respect him, it does say that he should love her as Christ loved the church. The wife is not called upon to demand that kind of love, but to keep her own love on as she honours the man she has married.

Too often in our society love is about what I expect or can demand from the other person. Too often the pursuit of love and indeed relationships and friendships generally seems to be primarily about me, what you can give me, what I want, my fulfillment, my satisfaction. It is not that these things are not very important in any relationship but, in terms of priorities, if it comes first, it can lead us astray quite badly. Outside marriage and friendships it can happen in many other areas, for example at work, or in church, or in our view of society. We can have an unbalanced expectation of what others should be doing for me, rather than what love may call me to be and do for them.

Where does thanksgiving come into this consideration of true love? Well I suggest that the more I notice, appreciate and thank the Lord for his absolutely incredible love and sacrifice for me, putting me first, in that while I was still a sinner Jesus died for me, (Romans 5:8); the more my love for Him will increase and the closer my experience of Him will become.

Secondly as I thank Him I will hear His call encouraging me to freely give because I have freely received, (Matthew 10:8), and to know that I can love like Jesus loved because He first loved me. (1 John 4:19). My giving in love will then have more energy and power in it, fueled by a recognition of His love and care for me, and a growing experience of the height, depth, length and width of this incredible love of God that 'surpasses knowledge'. (Ephesians 3:18, 19.)

Thirdly thanksgiving reminds me of all Christ's resources available to me, and within me, to be more able to love like Him. Added to this thanksgiving will remind me that love is a fruit of the Holy Spirit (Galatians 5:22) who is there to enable me, encourage me and flow with and through me in this. I am not trying to do it on my own.

Finally thanksgiving will help re-orientate my inner compass and priorities from any 'entitlement' temptation which can say 'what can I get'? or 'what's in it for me?', to finding a liberty to flow like Jesus in what I have to give to another in love.

Activation ...

As you give thanks today for every opportunity to demonstrate to the world the true meaning of love remember that you won't miss out, but you will discover more of the truth in the Lord's words, quoted by Paul to the elders of the church at Ephesus, Acts 20:35, *"It is more blessed to give than receive."*

DAY 236 | Thanksgiving for His Power Within

I had a dream last night, a strange dream. In it Mark and I were at a public swimming bath. When we got into the water, all the water mysteriously drained away. All the people in the pool were naturally perturbed, wondering where the water had gone, so we got out and as we did the water came back into the pool again. I was curious, so I went back to the pool side to see what would happen; to see if it was us that had caused this phenomenon, and sure enough, right by where I stood, the water started to recede from me. Satisfied that it was me that was causing this, I stood back again, thereby letting the water fill the swimming bath back up again.

I nearly dismissed this as just a random dream as I joked about it with Mark, but then I remembered that in the dream itself I had sensed that the water draining out of the pool was somehow a 'manifestation of the presence of God' and had felt quite excited by it. Then later as I looked in my journal I realised that the Lord was indeed speaking to me. In my journal I had been musing on the apostle John's encouragement to some early Christians about the spiritual battles they were in. Writing about the false spirits and the spirit of antichrist which he said was already in the world. He tells them, 'You are from God, little children, and have overcome them; because **greater is He who is in you than he who is in the world.**' (1 John 4:4.NASB)

Now I have always read that as an encouragement of a defensive kind, telling me that whatever comes against me won't overcome me because Jesus is within me, and He is bigger than anything that the world – or the devil – can throw at me. And this is true. However I realised, from the dream, that the Lord was saying something more. John's encouragement to the early church, living in a spiritually hostile world was about being on the **offensive**. It was not merely an encouragement about not being overcome by any enemy activity, but it was an encouragement that we God's children would be the overcomers of the enemy's activities, as we released God's kingdom into the world around us.

So going back to the dream I somehow knew, that the water represented the atmosphere in the world created by 'the prince of this world', (John 14:30). When we stepped into the pool that atmosphere drained away, because the atmosphere released from us, the presence of God from within us, was greater. I believe the Lord was saying that He wants us, His people, to realise how spiritually powerful we really are. We can, because the Lord is with us and in us, release His Kingdom blessings over people and places, thereby displacing the atmospheres and trouble created by the enemy.

Jesus expected that this would be true of the disciples when He sent them out two by two. He said to them, "When you enter a house, first say, 'Peace to this house.' If a man of peace is there, your peace will rest on him; if not, it will return to you." (Luke 10:5). Jesus was indicating that the disciples would be releasing the atmosphere of heaven – 'Peace' – and if it was welcomed it would make a difference. Now those disciples were operating under an anointing from the Lord, but had yet to be 'clothed with power from on high.' (Luke 24:49). Then after Pentecost the power being released from them was so great that people only had to come within shadow range of Peter to get healed. (Acts 5:15). God's indwelling power was spilling over from him, as it was from Paul, when cloth that had touched him, carried the healing presence of God to the sick. (Acts 19:12).

Does it all seem just too much to believe that God wants that same power to be manifested by His people today? Well I have deliberately quoted from the NASB, because it more accurately uses the Greek phrase 'little children'. We are God's 'little children', and so this is not about us feeling, big and brave, mature, clever, or even very spiritual. This is about us believing, like little children, that what our heavenly Father says is true, 'Greater is He that is in you than he who is in the world', and acting accordingly.

Activation . . .

Join me in believing that the Lord was speaking through this dream, and thank Him in every situation in which you find yourself today that, 'greater is He who is in you than he who is in the world'. As we do that I believe that we will begin to see some answers to our prayers, 'Your Kingdom come on earth, now, here and in this place, as it is in heaven.' Amen.

DAY 237 | Thanksgiving for God's Life in us

Thinking yesterday about the power of Jesus' life flowing from us, I was reminded of the promise that Jesus made in the Temple in Jerusalem. 'Jesus stood and cried out, saying, "If anyone is thirsty, let him come to me and drink. He who believes in me, as the scripture said, 'From his innermost being will flow rivers of living water.'" He was speaking of the Spirit, 'whom those who believed in Him were to receive; for the Spirit was not yet given, because Jesus was not yet glorified.' (John 7:37-39, NASB).

Maybe these words reminded Jesus' hearers of Ezekiel's vision of the River of God flowing from the Temple. This river got deeper and deeper bringing healing and life wherever it went. It even flowed into the Dead Sea, where nothing lives, and brought 'life'. Ezekiel wrote of the river saying, *'When it empties into the sea, (Dead Sea) the water there becomes fresh. Swarms of living creatures will live wherever the river flows. There will be large numbers of fish, because this water flows there and makes the salt water fresh; so wherever the water flows everything will live.'* (Ezekiel 47:1-9).

These two passages illustrate to me the power of the life of God that Jesus said would flow from a believer, bringing the life of God into dead places, displacing the atmosphere of the 'the prince of this world', (John 14:30). It is something that Jesus did time and time again, like He did for the woman caught in adultery. With one statement He changed the atmosphere around that woman from hatred, fear, vindictiveness and condemnation, to peace, mercy, forgiveness and restoration. (John 8:1-11). How wonderful is that? And He did that time and time again.

We know, however, that not everyone welcomes the invasion of this 'river of life' into their world, because Jesus Himself made some people very angry. They accused Him of being demon possessed, (John 8:48); tried to seize Him, (John 10:39), and of course eventually the power and the goodness flowing from Him so enraged them that they called for His crucifixion, and the whipped up crowd, that day, chose death in the form of Barabbus, rather than the life that was flowing from Jesus. (Matthew 27:21).

Peter and Paul, who were used so powerfully to release this life changing river of life, also suffered. There was imprisonment and floggings, (Acts 5:33-40, Acts 12:1-5, and Acts 14:19). Stephen was actually stoned to death as he preached. The point is this, carrying the presence of God, and releasing the river of life, can change lives and whole situations, but it can also bring opposition. The question then is, if 'greater is He that is in you, than he who is in the world,' why do these things happen, and evil seem to win?

Well let's look at this a little closer. When Stephen died, his enemies may have won an earthly victory, but 'Stephen, full of the Holy Spirit, looked up into heaven and saw the glory of God, and Jesus standing at the right hand of God'. He was able to pray for his killers as Jesus did, "Lord, do not hold this sin against them". (Acts 7:54-59). Was this what Paul meant when he wrote, 'But thanks be to God, who always leads us in triumphal procession in Christ and through us spreads everywhere the fragrance of the knowledge of Him. For we are to God the aroma of Christ ... To the one we are a smell of death; to the other, the fragrance of life.' (2 Corinthians 2:14-16).

To quote Bob Mumford again, 'to insist we will always come out on top of every difficult circumstance is neither biblical nor realistic'.[1] We might not always see an earthly 'victory', but God's heart is that, in the challenges of life, we will find ourselves to be, 'more than a conqueror through Him who loved us.' (Romans 8:35-37), as we let His life and love flow through us.

Activation ...

Today's encouragement is therefore to keep thanking the Lord, even in those difficult and seemingly irresolvable situations. Thank Him that His life **is** flowing from you. Thank Him that His life can flow, and bring life, even into the 'dead sea' places that we encounter. Let us, even where there is opposition or rejection, keep thanking Him that He is with us. Let us keep releasing His blessing, and let Him lead us 'in triumph' His way – the way that will bring Him the most glory.

DAY 238 | Thanksgiving that Keeps us Flexible!

A while ago now I bought a small Monkey Puzzle tree, for Mark. We like Monkey Puzzle trees and, although we know they are slow growing, we were looking forward to watching it grow into a tall and majestic tree. We replanted it into a very large pot, to give its roots plenty of room to grow and become established and then, when it didn't seem to be gaining much height, we put it into the ground with much care and lots of good compost.

It did grow then, mainly outwards. Time went on and it still didn't gain height. We realized, on examination, (not easy, they are very prickly) that it had more than one main trunk. It was in fact a 'Monkey Puzzle bush'. I know! That's strange isn't it? So while admiring other Monkey Puzzle trees for their impressive height and elegance, I have been walking past our tree day by day wondering if, and when, it will grow tall and strong. So rather slowly I have been coming to terms with the realization and disappointment that this bush is not what I had hoped for.

This morning, however, as I stepped outside and walked past our tree, the sun was catching the fresh green of the new growth on it, (which always seems to be out sideways!!) and it actually looked really stunning. Not what I had originally bargained for, but unexpectedly beautiful in its own way. It was then that I felt one of those 'whispers' from God. "If you will give me thanks, even when things don't seem to be what you think they should be, you will 'see' things through My eyes and recognise what I am doing, sometimes in ways that you don't expect."

I felt that the Lord was encouraging me not to be too rigid in my expectations. He was saying in effect, "Stay flexible in how you 'see' things. Let Me show you how I see things, or you may miss the beauty in what I am doing." If our mental picture of what something should look like is not flexible we will be discontent and miss some real blessings, and even worse, if it's about another person, we may well rob another of our honour and esteem.

I am thinking here of the minister who comes to a church, and because he or she doesn't fit the frame that the members of that church have for him or her, the minister can feel criticised, or just not what is wanted. If that leads to discouragement, they may well become less fruitful in their ministry. At the same time the church members may never get to enjoy the benefits of what the minister **does** have to offer, or experience the joy of him/her blossoming in his/her particular gifting.

We can all see how hard and sad that is, but this can actually happen in our lives in all sorts of ways and with all sorts of people and situations. Where we have a set idea of how something should be, or how it should look, we can be focusing on what something **isn't** and miss what it **is**, or **could be** for us. As with me and our tree, focusing on what something or someone **isn't**; on how someone, or something, doesn't fit our expectations, can prevent us from seeing what **is** there, what **is** beautiful and what **is** a blessing.

Giving thanks for people, places, and events of all sorts, keeps us flexible in our thinking and expectations. Thanksgiving helps us to better see what **'is'** and be less preoccupied with what **'isn't'**. I think this may be another angle on the advice Paul gave to the Philippians, 'Finally, brothers, whatever is true, whatever is noble, whatever is right, whatever is pure, whatever is lovely, whatever is admirable – if anything is excellent or praiseworthy – think about such things.' (Philippians 4:8).

I can think of no better way to keep my mind focused on those 'excellent and praiseworthy' kinds of things, and away from focusing on lack, leading to disappointment, than giving thanks. Thanksgiving helps me not to get too narrow and inflexible, and it helps me to share God's big heart and amazing perspective on all kinds of things. It's a powerful way to keep our minds flexible and open to all that the Lord has for us in a situation, in a friendship, or in a relationship.

Activation ...

Let your heart of gratitude for 'what is', enable you to see life through the right lens so that you don't miss those hidden blessings – like trees that are actually bushes, but are nevertheless very beautiful!

DAY 239 | Thanksgiving and the Unexpected

Yesterday we reflected on how easy it is to have fixed expectations of events, other people, and what God is, or should be doing and how that can cause us to focus on what doesn't seem good about a situation, how someone isn't living up to our expectations, or what it seems God isn't doing. So today let's have a look, at C S Lewis's revelation that although Jesus may appear unpredictable, yet He is always good.

In the Lion, the Witch and the Wardrobe, that magnificent book for adults that children enjoy too, the four children have a conversation with Mr and Mrs Beaver in the beaver's house. It's beautiful and it contains some wonderful truth because C S Lewis had a marvelous way of describing profound things about the Lord, and His ways with us, through allegory. The children are asking the Beavers about Aslan (who is a picture of Jesus). They have never met, or heard of Him before, and have just been told that He is a lion, a great lion. "Is He safe?" asks Susan. "Safe?" said Mr. Beaver; "don't you hear what Mrs. Beaver tells you? Who said anything about safe? 'Course he isn't safe. But he's good. He's the King, I tell you." Then, towards the end of the story, they remember Mr Beaver's words: "...He's wild, you know. Not like a *tame* lion."[1]

Maybe in the relative comfort of the west we have allowed ourselves to be confused about the word 'safe'. Undoubtedly the Lord is our sure place of safety. "The name of the Lord is a strong tower; the righteous run into it and is safe." (Proverbs 18:10, NASB). However if by safe we are thinking 'predictable', 'doing it my way', or 'the way I have been taught to expect,' we could be in for some surprises and even some perplexity because the Lord is not, in that sense, our 'tame' Lord. When Jesus was on earth the expectations of those trying to follow Him were often shaken. If we had been around, we might have heard some conversations which loosely put might have gone something like this:-

~ John the Baptist, "I expected you to get me out of prison (He had heard the declaration recorded for us in Luke 4:18), but you haven't." (and He didn't) Jesus response was, "Don't be offended." (Luke 7:18 onwards).

- Peter, "There is revival in town, everyone wants to hear you. Stay and reap a great harvest." Jesus, "No I must move on." (Mark 1:32-38).
- Jesus brother's, "You are the Messiah, go up to the city and make yourself fully known – you need publicity." (That is have a big campaign so everyone knows the Messiah is here). Jesus, "no – not yet". (John 7:1-9).
- Peter, "Very big spiritual event here on Mount of transfiguration – must build a suitable monument to commemorate/attract people." Father God, "(No) Just listen to my Son." (Mark 9:5-7).
- Peter, "God forbid it Lord! This shall never happen to you." (That's not right, the Messiah can't die,). Jesus, "You don't understand God's plan and ways Peter. Your expectations are all wrong." (Matthew 16:21-23).
- People in Nazareth, "Great miracles, great wisdom, but hang on! He grew up here, we know him and His family." Expectations hit by offence, giving rise to unbelief and very little blessing. (Mark 6:1-6).
- Disciples (**After** the resurrection), "Will you now restore the kingdom to Israel (and get rid of the Romans)?" Jesus, "(Not the right expectation boys!) Stay in Jerusalem and await the Holy Spirit coming upon you when you will receive power and be my witnesses." They expected a major external event to mightily change life for everyone. God had planned a major personal event for them all, to mightily change their lives which would then flow outwards and change others. (Acts 1:6-8).

All of us carry expectations of how things should be. The more we take time to 'chew' on His goodness and love with thanksgiving, the easier it will be to see His hand and ways in the unexpected, the disappointments and the perplexities of life. Then our faith will grow, as we see what God **is** doing, and what good **is** being worked in a situation for us and others.

Activation . . .

When your expectations aren't met let thanksgiving help you to focus on, and stay with the absolute truths that God is good, and God is love. Thanksgiving is a great way to 'chew the cud', and get the nourishment from these truths like cows in a field chewing the cud. As you give thanks over and over, you will come to a more settled place of faith. Then the perplexities of unfulfilled expectations have a safe context. Remember – it was only ok that Aslan was not 'safe' or 'tame' because He was also all love and goodness.

DAY 240 | Thanksgiving and Staying Malleable!

In the book of Isaiah, we read of God speaking to His people prophetically, and also of the prophet Isaiah, responding to God's words and praying for His nation. At one point he reminds God of all the times when He did amazing things to rescue His people, and then he acknowledges the bad state that they have got themselves into. He says to God, 'No one calls on your name or strives to lay hold of you; for you have hidden your face from us and made us waste away because of our sins.' (Isaiah 64:7).

Whilst acknowledging God's right to judge them at this time, he reminds God of who He is for them. He writes, 'Yet, O Lord, you are our Father. We are the clay, you are the potter; we are all the work of your hand.' (Isaiah 64:8). It's a picture God also used with the prophet Jeremiah, telling him to go and watch the potter at work. When the potter found a problem in the clay, he started again with the clay and reshaped it into another pot. God's word to Jeremiah was this, "O house of Israel, can I not do with you as this potter does? Like clay in the hands of the potter, so are you in my hand.' (Jeremiah 18:6).

So there it is, He is the potter and we are the clay, no argument there. We are God's people and He has the right to mould and shape us as He pleases. There are however, for us, some important differences. Firstly, when these words were written, they were written to an apostate nation under judgment. We know that for us, Jesus has taken all the judgment, and now it's all about transformation, it's about being 'conformed to the likeness' of that same Jesus. (Romans 8:29)

God is still the potter and we the clay, but now the moulding is not primarily to bring us back into line, or to prevent us from turning away, it is in order to grow the 'new us' into the image of Jesus. We can behold Jesus, and know and understand what the Lord is after in His 'moulding' of us. 'But we know that when He appears, we shall be like Him, for we shall see Him as He is.' (1 John 3:2). And until then, while we are on earth in this life, we can rejoice that we are already on that journey of being 'changed into the same image from glory to glory, *even* as by the Spirit of the Lord.' (2 Corinthians 3:18, AV).

Isaiah rightly pointed out to God that He was also 'Father' of the nation, as well as being 'the Potter'. For us God's fatherhood applies to us as individuals because we have been adopted into God's family through Christ, and have His Spirit within crying *"Abba* Father." (Romans 8:15). Simply put, the 'potter', the one whose hands are moulding us, is our Abba, our Daddy. Our Father who loves us to bits.

We also know from that same verse, that the lovely Holy Spirit, (just look at His characteristics in Galatians 5:22,23.) is the One who is at work in us to change and mould us. I am just so glad that Father God doesn't delegate this amazing work to any spiritual being other than the third member of the Trinity. We are changed 'from glory to glory, **even as by the Spirit of the Lord**'. (2 Corinthians 3:18). So Father, Son and Holy Spirit are all working together for my good and God's glory.

Over the last few months we have often written of the connection between thanksgiving and being transformed to look like Jesus, and we have made countless reference to how thanksgiving enables us to stay connected to the Lord in so many different scenarios. Today let us express our gratitude that the potter's hands that are moulding us, are the very hands of our loving heavenly Father, who is working to make us like Jesus, by the power of the indwelling Holy Spirit. Let us be thankful that all three members of the Trinity are in complete agreement, and are working for our transformation.

Activation ...

Let your thanksgiving today keep you 'soft' and malleable in His hands, thereby making you easier to mould. Your thanksgiving denotes, both to God, and indeed to your own spirit, that you are seeking to cooperate in this process. That will make the moulding easier for God ... and for you !!

DAY 241 | Thanksgiving and our Communication with 'The Potter'

Yesterday we were sharing the truth that God is like the potter to our clay, and we were reminding ourselves that the hands that are moulding us are not the hands of just any potter; these are the hands of our loving heavenly Father. We need to know that although God uses the picture of 'clay in the hands of the potter', it does not mean that God treats us literally like a lump of clay, something He just forces into the shape that He wants.

We need to know with a certainty that God is making us beautiful through a relationship that is saturated with His love for us. We know that our God is supremely into relationship, because every page of the bible shouts at us that our God is a relational being. Even at the beginning we read, 'Then God said, "Let **us** make man in **our** image, after **our** likeness"'. (Genesis 1:26). This epically creative moment was talked about and shared within the Trinity; Father, Son and Holy Spirit. Since they made us 'in their image', we too are relational beings.

All three members of the Godhead want to be in an ongoing relationship with us, and relationship involves communication and dialogue. This is why we worship, pray, talk and listen to God whenever we can. Sometimes we have been taught that submitting to God means that we never question Him. Questioning God, you might remember, didn't go down too well for Job as his questions exposed his own heart and the limits of his understanding of the Lord's ways, so God challenged him to answer **His** questions instead. (Job 38:1-3). Although in the end Job has that wonderful revelation of God, (Job 42:1-3) it is still a cautionary tale of attitudes that can hinder our communication with the Lord.

This is important because God wants there to be a growing relationship between us and Him. We are His dearly loved children, (1 John 3:1) and good parenting involves loving, listening and dialogue, as well as direction and correction. God does not want His 'moulding' of us to take place by force, or even fear, but out of our response to His love and care. We need therefore to be free to ask questions, but they need to be the right ones.

I think we all know, that 'Why' questions are often not helpful. Asked in the wrong way they can merely put us into a victim frame of mind. The 'Why me?' 'Why is this happening?' 'Why doesn't God ... ?' sort of questions. The ones that God didn't answer for Job. However when we ask the right sort of questions with hopeful trust in our hearts, relationship is built.

One of the keys, I believe, to asking the right question, with the right attitude of heart, is thanksgiving. So for example when we are perplexed, or confused, instead of just praying, 'Help, God get me out of here, why is this happening? Please Lord do something . . .', we can talk to the Lord something like this. 'Father I am feeling quite distressed by this situation but I thank you that you are with me, and I thank you that you said in your word you would give wisdom generously to those who ask.' (James 1:5). (No need to quote chapter and verse to the Lord!!!). 'What is your purpose here Lord? What would you like me to do?' or, 'What blessings are you looking to release into this situation?'

I think God loves our How? When? What? Where? and Who? questions. They delight His heart. He loves our cooperation, even our partnership in the 'moulding' process. Like little children who love to explore and learn, let us approach Him with thanksgiving and ask our questions believing that He loves to lead and guide us and that He will be only too ready to speak into our hearts and lives, sharing with us all that He knows we need to know in each situation.

Activation . . .

Try to ask the right sort of questions today, and don't be surprised at the ways in which the Lord speaks back to you!

These could be questions like, *'What would you like me to do here Lord?' What 'fruit' are you 'growing' in me through this circumstance Lord? 'How would you like me to bless this person?' 'What is the promise, or who is the person that will help me with this problem?'* These are good ones, and they will help you to grow and mature in your different circumstances, and thereby to grow in your friendship with the Lord.

DAY 242 | Thanksgiving and our Communication with our Heavenly Father

Yesterday we were thinking about the right and wrong kinds of questions that we can ask in our conversations with God. We made the statement that 'Why?' questions are often not helpful, but we do need to qualify this because even a 'Why?' question can be helpful if it is asked with faith in our hearts. Asking "Why is this happening?" as I seek understanding and insight is so different to asking, "Why is this happening to me?" from a place in my heart of 'It's not fair'. So now we have a further understanding of why starting our conversation with God with thanksgiving is a very good thing, because if we do give thanks first, we can even ask a 'why?' question as it will be mixed with faith and expectancy

We read in Hebrews that '... without faith it is impossible to please God, because anyone who comes to him must believe that he exists and that he rewards those who earnestly seek Him.' (Hebrews 11:6). The rest of that chapter lists numbers of people who are remembered as people of faith, who have seen God do amazing things with, and for them, on their journey through life. They have by no means been perfect, they have made mistakes, but in the 'Faith Hall of Fame', they are remembered for the deliverances and miracles they have seen.

Often those deliverances and miracles occurred because those people found themselves in difficult, disappointing, or even terrifying circumstances. They were in situations where their faith had to grow beyond the circumstances in which they found themselves. No doubt many of them had questions to ask of God, even the 'Why?' ones! We don't know how those conversations went, but we do know that they were entered into that list of 'Faith Heroes', so they must have believed that God existed and that He would reward them as they sought for His help.

In our own lives we are more likely to ask questions of God when things are tough, because it is in these situations that we can feel bewildered.

Thanksgiving will always help us, in those seasons, to make that shift in our attitude from bewilderment to a place of faith. Intentionally thanking God for His love and grace helps to shift our mindset to a place of believing that the Lord is in this situation, and will be working in it for our good.

Coming to God with thanksgiving expresses my faith in God that He is wanting to guide and help me through these times, and because relationship is paramount to God I can then approach Him in faith with my 'Why?' questions. My thanksgiving is an expression of my faith in God's goodness and my belief that He will want to answer me and to dialogue with me as He did with David. It is all about knowing that He loves to give wisdom and grace to those who ask.

There are times of course when God doesn't seem inclined to answer any of our questions at all. Maybe as He did with Job, He will have questions for us to answer first. It is important in these times that we keep our eyes on Him and stay in faith looking to God for how and in what way He is communicating with us. Our continued thanksgiving at these times will help us to discern what God is working in our lives, and will also help us to 'hear' what the Lord has to say back to us ... Something on which we will ponder further tomorrow.

Activation ...

Next time you feel a "Why God?" question arising in your heart, intentionally turn to Him with thanksgiving for His goodness and love, and for His help in previous situations. Then notice how this shifts your "why?" question from a possible complaint, to one of faith filled enquiry.

DAY 243 | Hearing the Lord's Response to me

For the last couple of days we have been looking at prayer not just as 'asking' God to do something for us, but as a dialogue, wherein we can ask Him questions and seek His wisdom in our circumstances and situations. We have suggested that if we begin our dialogue with God with thanksgiving, it will help us to ask with faith in our hearts, which of course pleases God.

The next important thing to ponder is, 'How I am expecting to receive God's response to me?' and we use the word 'response' because we don't always get the direct reply from God that we would like. When we ask our questions we need to remember that He is not on the stand in a court of law, rather He is the potter and we are the clay – so let's stay humble.

Sometimes the Lord answers us immediately as we read our Bible. He may, at other times bring to mind a scripture or a sermon that we heard, reminding us of a truth we have been taught, or a testimony we have heard. At other times there is a delay, and at these times especially, thanksgiving keeps us in faith and expectant that the Lord has heard our prayer/questions, and that the Holy Spirit is seeking to show us the answer, or the way ahead, in His own time and way.

To ask and then expect an immediate answer can be faith destroying, but to ask and then trust is far better. I think that sometimes an immediate answer from the Lord is not possible because we don't have the right understanding or maturity within ourselves to actually discern what He is saying. We often therefore receive the Lord's response to us through another's teaching or prophesy, or as we talk with other Christians. It is often as we share together with other believers that we find the mind of Christ. (1 Corinthians 2:15,16): A good reason to meet regularly with others who believe.

Not only will we not necessarily get an immediate answer, it is also rare for us to hear the audible voice of God, though clearly some people have. The Lord can of course speak to us through dreams and visions, but I think that more often He wants us to hear His voice in a simpler, more straight forward, way through our own thinking as we ponder a matter. These thoughts are best informed by our knowledge and understanding of the Bible which is why it is important that we keep reading and absorbing all that the Lord shows us of Himself through His 'Word', the Bible.

We also have the indwelling Spirit of God living with us and so, often, these answers to our questions will come to us as we worship and praise the Lord opening ourselves up to the Spirit of God who delights to 'lead us into all truth'. (John 16:13). There can often be that 'aha' moment, that inner witness and recognition as our spirit agrees with the Holy Spirit. (We may also recognise sometimes that, left to our own devices, we would never ourselves have thought that thought).

One verse that always comes to mind when thinking about prayer is Philippians 4:6, 7, 'Do not be anxious about anything, but in everything, by prayer and petition, with thanksgiving, present your requests to God. And the peace of God, which transcends all understanding, will guard your hearts and your minds in Christ Jesus.' Thanking the Lord for His love and presence with us, keeps us open to receive what he has to say. His answers come in many varied and even unexpected ways, and when they come they also bring us His peace.

i) God the Holy Spirit will always speak to us truths that will accord with scripture. This does not mean that every prompting of the Spirit will come with a biblical verse, or precedent, but He will never lead us in a way that violates all that He has revealed of Himself in His Word.

ii) The Lord's 'voice' may be correctional but it will not be shaming and condemning. If He is speaking to us about something that is wrong, He will always point us to the cross, where we can find grace and forgiveness,

iii) If this whole process of communicating with the Lord is soaked in thanksgiving, it will increase my faith, enable me to hear Him more clearly and it will also help me not to fall into error, because as I 'test out' what I believe I am hearing, (may be by sharing it with a trusted friend), continuing in thanksgiving will bring a sense of harmony and peace to my mind and heart.

DAY 244 | Thanksgiving and God's Moment by Moment Provision

In John's gospel we read of an encounter that Jesus had with a Samaritan woman at a well. (John 4:4-26). Jesus, as He often seems to, avoids her question and makes a strong statement of His own. The dialogue, after Jesus has asked for a drink, goes thus – Samaritan woman, "You are a Jew and I am a Samaritan woman. How can you ask me for a drink?" Jesus answers, "If you knew the gift of God and who it is that asks you for a drink, you would have asked him and he would have given you living water." It's that phrase **"if you knew the gift of God and who it is who asked . . ."** that drew my attention. I thought how often we have a question in our hearts that we'd like to ask God, and He seems to avoid giving us an answer, but then hints that He has something else to give us.

It's interesting to note that it was not in our 21st century world that this conversation took place, but two thousand years ago, and this woman raises the issues of sexism and racism, stalling a bit I think, because she is shocked that Jesus, a Jewish man, would even speak to her, let alone ask for her help. Jesus didn't then take the opportunity to teach her that in His new Kingdom there would be neither male nor female, slave nor free, Jew nor gentile (Greek). (Galatians 3:28). Instead He provokes her with two things that would be more important to her in that moment. **Firstly He hints that He is someone special, and secondly that He has something to give her.**

Don't you just love watching the way Jesus is with different people in their differing needs and conditions? It is wonderful to observe, but more than that, seeing how He was with people when He was on earth can help us in those times when we don't understand what is happening, or what He is doing in our own lives. When we are in a situation, and it appears that the Lord either hasn't heard our prayer, or isn't inclined to answer our questions, we need to hear again what He said to the Samaritan woman. He provoked her to consider two things. i) **Who He is**, and ii) **what gift He has to give.**

Let's consider a real life situation. I am feeling afraid for some reason. It could be about money, my job, my reputation, the family, my health or in fact any area of life where my wellbeing is threatened in some way. I ask the Lord to deal with it, change things, rescue me, intervene in some way, but not a lot happens. I may even find that the ways in which He used to intervene when I was first saved don't seem to be happening anymore. I now believe that this is because the Lord is more interested in my relationship with Him than in providing me with a quick fix. He is looking to grow me and each one of us up into 'mature sonship'. (cf. Romans 8:19).

So if I take account of the two things mentioned above and speak to myself about i) **who He is for me**, and ii) **what gift He might have for me**, I will pray in a different, more faith filled way. And yes! Yet again, thanksgiving will play a big part. I remind myself and thank Him for **who He is for me**; My loving heavenly Father, (Matthew 6:25-34), My strong deliverer, (Psalm 18:2), My provider, (Psalm 23:1), My very present help in trouble (Psalm 46:1). It's a time to take the names of God — who He has declared Himself to be — and personalise those names, with thanksgiving, for me in my current situation.

Then, I can go on with rising faith and expectancy, fuelled by my thanksgiving, to perceive **what gift He might have for me** in that situation; His peace, His wisdom, His joy, His friendship, His deliverance, His forgiveness, patience, provision, healing or strength etc, etc. He will always have a relevant grace gift for me, because that is the kind of heavenly Father that He is. I can then recognise and receive those gifts with a thankful heart.

Activation ...

Next time you are feeling threatened by a situation, use it as a wonderful opportunity to grow closer to God, and to discover more about His love, **who He is for you in this situation and what He has to give you.** Grasp the opportunity to 'taste and see that the Lord is good'. (Psalm 34:8). Remember Eugene Peterson's paraphrase in The Message of Romans 8:16,17, and as you give Him your thanks become, 'adventurously expectant' in your life with God saying, "What's next Papa?" What gift have you got to give to me for this situation? ... and the next one? ... and this one? ... and the next ... until it becomes a lifestyle full of expectant faith.

DAY 245 | Thanksgiving and Celebration

It occurred to me the other day that our God is a God who loves celebration. He particularly loves it when His people recognise what He has done for them and choose to celebrate enthusiastically. It always seems a bit strange to me that a vast crowd of people can go wild and celebrate when a piece of leather in the shape of a ball is landed in the back of a net, and yet Christians who get excited about the Lord and all that He has done for them are called 'fanatics'.

The other somewhat strange thing that has happened in our society is the 'cult of celebrity'. It's the practice of calling someone a celebrity when they may just have achieved notoriety through some television program, or even through some misdemeanor or other. They become celebrities and their opinions about all sorts of issues are canvassed while others, the real celebrities of life, like the care workers and huge numbers of volunteer charity workers often go unnoticed.

A group of us a while back were reading through the book of Ruth together, and it occurred to me that Ruth was just an ordinary person who chose, after great personal tragedy, to stay loyal to her mother-in-law. This caused her to leave her country, give up her chance of remarriage, and become the sole breadwinner for herself and an older woman in a land where, as a single woman, she was a foreigner, very vulnerable and, should Naomi die, very alone. (Ruth 2:1-9).

We know the wonderful end to Ruth's story; how she married Boaz and gave birth to Obed, David's grandfather, and how she, a Moabitess appears, (very unusually for a woman and a gentile), in the genealogy of Jesus in Matthew 1:5-17. Ruth has been celebrated through the years as a great woman of God. Her story has been told and read over and over, but she was just an ordinary woman making some good choices, and doing the Godly thing in an unknown small village in the tiny country of Israel.

As we read this story, and I looked around the room, it occurred to me that all our stories will be told in heaven. Each one of us will be celebrated for what we have done, things seen and unseen, acknowledged and unacknowledged by the world. God sees and so do the 'great cloud of witnesses' that surround us (Hebrews 12:1). I believe that there is celebration and cheering in heaven not just on the day when we turned to Jesus, (Luke 15:7), but every time we bring glory to Jesus, by living from our 'New Life' in Him, every time we choose His way, and allow the Holy Spirit to produce that beautiful Christ like fruit in our lives.

This then gives us reason to thank Him for every opportunity we get, like Ruth, to declare that we will choose His way, even when it seems tough, (Ruth 1:16,17), and against what we would really like to do. It's about His Lordship in our lives. Making Him Lord and not just Saviour makes us celebrities from heaven's perspective, those who are, and will be, celebrated in heaven.

Activation...

If you can give thanks for this amazing truth it will transform the most mundane and ordinary day into something special. It can make you aware of how important your day to day choices can be in terms of eternal values. Heavenly values are so different to those of this world, and it's probably no mistake that Mother Theresa's biography was called 'Something Beautiful for God'. So let us thank Him every time we have an opportunity to do something that is 'beautiful', from heavens perspective, and let us bring Jesus much glory everyday of our lives.

DAY 246 | Thanksgiving that Jesus is the 'door'

During the recent pandemic, many of us experienced 'shut doors', places where access was denied. At the height of the 'lockdowns' this affected care homes, churches, playgrounds, and pubs. Even some whole countries shut their doors. All this gave rise to the wonderful thought that our access to God is never denied or even limited *because Jesus is the 'door'*.

In one of Jesus' 'I AM' statements, (which makes it of great significance), He said, "I am the Door; anyone who enters in through Me will be saved (will live). He will come in and he will go out (freely), and will find pasture." (John 10:9, AMP). Now going through a door signifies a transition; a shift from one location to another. In this life we can only be in one place at a time, and a door therefore signifies a change, a leaving of one place, or room, and an entering into another.

Jesus knew that He was going to be the entrance point, 'the Door', through which mankind could come into God's presence for all eternity, because He was going to remove the 'virus'– our sin, the thing that would ban us from entry. In Hebrews 9 and 10, we have a wonderful description of how Jesus, our High Priest, has made a way for us all to enter in to the Holy of Holies, God's very presence, through His own blood. The writer concludes – 'Therefore, brothers, since we have confidence to enter into the Most Holy Place by the blood of Jesus, by a new and living way opened up for us through the curtain, that is, His body ... let us draw near to God with a sincere heart in full assurance of faith, having our hearts sprinkled to cleanse us from a guilty conscience ...' (Hebrews 10:19-22).

Our 'accuser' the devil, however, will always point to our 'filthy rags' as he did with Joshua the High Priest. (Zechariah 3:1-5). He will always try to get us to believe that we are still 'outside' of God's presence. God's response was to rebuke Satan and get Joshua a change of clothes. A divine exchange; rich garments and a clean turban for those 'filthy rags', and that is exactly what He has done for us. Spiritually, we have already transitioned. We are now citizens of heaven. God has, 'rescued us from the dominion of darkness and brought us into the kingdom of the Son He loves.' (Colossians 1:13).

God has, 'raised us up with Christ and seated us with Him in the heavenly realms in Christ Jesus ...' (Ephesians 2:6), and He has already, '... blessed us in the heavenly realms with every spiritual blessing in Christ.' (Ephesians 1:3).

That is the spiritual reality, but even though we know these truths, we too find ourselves troubled by the 'accuser' who endeavors to resurrect our guilty consciences, and make us feel that we are back in his domain. Often when we seek to come to the Lord in worship or prayer, we find ourselves thinking. "I haven't done so good today." "I haven't read the bible very much." "I'm feeling full of doubt." "God won't be happy with me today." On and on he goes with his accusations,

The picture I have in my mind however, is of Jesus, standing as the 'Door' of the heavenly throne room, and as we approach He has a big smile of welcome. He has in His hand a beautiful robe of righteousness which He just delights to give us in exchange for whatever 'filthy rags' that we feel we have on today. As we approach God through Jesus, our 'door', we get to take off our 'sin stuff', and even our own righteousness, (Isaiah 64:6), and in exchange we get a robe of righteousness, His righteousness. (Isaiah 61:10). I hope this picture can help us to appropriate this truth in the moment, day by day, because God never ever wants us to feel that we are going to be denied access to that Holy place, because He's already paid the price for our new beautiful garments; they are, in fact, already ours if we are 'in Christ'.

How do we get our minds and hearts to catch up with this reality? The key is 'thanksgiving'. As I give thanks for these beautiful clean garments, my mind gets into line with the spiritual truths we have been sharing. Thanking Jesus for our new clothes defeats the enemy, it sends him packing with his accusations and it releases our faith that, however unworthy we feel, access to the Holy of Holies is never going to be denied us because we are 'clothed in His righteousness'.

Activation ...

Take some time to meditate on, and give thanks today for, these words from Isaiah 61:10. *'I delight greatly in the Lord; my soul rejoices in my God. For He has clothed me with garments of Salvation and arrayed me in a robe of righteousness.'*

DAY 247 | Thanksgiving that is Active

Today's thought is around the idea that 'thanksgiving' can be active or, in polite society, something that is almost passive. Maybe someone in your household has borrowed a book or something impersonal and, in passing, they put it back on the table by you, saying casually, "By the way there's that book I borrowed a while back." Because it really isn't something, the return of which you have been eagerly awaiting, you barely look up but just acknowledge with a polite, "Oh thanks, I wondered where that was."

Now compare that to someone in a desert offered some life saving water. The response there is going to be very different. Their thank you will probably be stifled by the grabbing of the water bottle from your hand, and the taking of their first gulps. I guess the depth of our gratitude will be in proportion to our hunger for the thing being given, or offered, and our hunger will also probably determine how 'active' our thanks is.

I think of Bartimaeus, (Mark 10:46-52), or the lame man at the gate Beautiful who, after He was healed, went about 'walking and jumping and praising God.' (Acts 3:1-8). And what about Mary and Martha after Lazarus was raised from the dead, (John 11:1-45)? We are not told about the party they may have had that evening, as all their neighbours and friends gathered to witness the miracle. Suffice it to say that when there has been a measure of desperation, the gratitude expressed is going to be great.

Then we read about the ten lepers that were healed, 'One of them, when he saw that he was healed, came back, praising God in a loud voice. He threw himself at Jesus' feet and thanked him ...' (Luke 17:15,16). Apparently the other nine took their healing for granted. Remember that you too were a leper spiritually speaking, excluded by your sin from God's presence, but you have been 'healed' and are now part of God's Kingdom with all the benefits and blessings that that affords.

So I need to ask myself what about me? I just feel that there are so many things that I take for granted. Like the fact that Jesus is always there when I want to talk to Him; that there is always forgiveness whenever I have need of it, and there is always help from our 'Helper' the Holy Spirit, any time of the day or night. Because as we have commented in these meditations – there is a bigness in God's heart to give and give, and give again, if I am ready and eager to receive what He offers.

We need to understand the joy that we can have in giving 'thanks' back to our giving God. Therefore I don't want that thanksgiving to be routine, nominal or just a passive 'Oh thanks.' I want my 'thanksgiving' to be active, not just polite. I want it to be accompanied by a taking hold of whatever it is God is offering in each moment. Let us not leave His grace and His gifts to us on the table, like that book that we really didn't particularly need back at that moment. Let us make our thanksgiving the active kind, the kind that our grandson expresses as he rips open the parcel containing the Lego present he has asked for, longed for and waited impatiently for, and which he knows is inside the wrapping.

Nobody told the lame man to jump and leap and praise God. He did so because that healing made a life changing difference. And as we appreciate the magnitude of the difference He has made, and is making, in our lives, this will be reflected in the way we express our gratitude. God wants us, 'walking and jumping and praising' Him, not because He thinks that we need the physical exercise, but because He will know, by our thanksgiving, that we have truly recognised His love, His generosity and His hand on our lives. It is therefore good sometimes, to ask the Holy Spirit to keep us mindful of the difference that all the grace we receive daily makes to our lives. To even consider where we might be, had it not been for His interventions of love and mercy in our lives. Then our recognition of the difference that He has made will be reflected in our thanksgiving

---

Activation . . .

Tune your heart today to be like the one leper who returned to give Jesus thanks and intentionally give the Lord your 'heartfelt' thanks whenever you can, as you grasp just how much He has already given you, and that He still is, pouring into your life His love and grace, moment by moment.

DAY 248 | Thanksgiving and Sacrifice

I feel excited about today's reflections, because I believe it is in God's heart to give us an invitation. One that I hope we won't be able to refuse.

So! Talking about personal 'sacrifice' is not likely to draw a crowd. Sacrifice is often associated with death, like in a war we speak of those who have 'made the ultimate sacrifice'. More generally, in the world at large, being sacrificial carries the implication that I won't get my own way in a situation or a relationship. I have even heard recently that 'sacrifice' is now getting a bad press, and that far from denoting heroism, it is being aligned to being 'walked over', 'suppressed' or 'not being your own person'.

We know that Jesus made the ultimate sacrifice. His coming to earth, to our world, was sacrificial in itself, (Philippians 2:5-11). Then He offered His life for the sin of the whole world. He was the Sacrificial Lamb of God. His death on the cross was the price for our forgiveness, and we were then given His righteousness in exchange for those 'filthy rags' that we were talking about the day before yesterday. His sacrificial death has made the way for us to enter into His world. He paid the price for our access to the throne room of heaven itself, both now in this life, and for eternity when we die.

So, 'in view of God's mercy', Paul urges the Christians in Rome, 'offer your bodies as living sacrifices, holy and pleasing to God – this is your spiritual act of worship. Do not be conformed to the pattern of this world, but be transformed by the renewing of your mind. Then you will be able to test and approve what God's will is – his good, pleasing and perfect will.' (Romans 12:1,2). So there we have it, we can't earn our salvation, Jesus the sacrificial Lamb has already paid the price for that, but we are invited here, in view of God's mercy, to 'offer' something back to God, and that something is our whole lives to be a 'Living Sacrifice'.

Now I don't know about you, but presenting my body as a living sacrifice, can feel scary. It held me up a bit after I had become a Christian, because my fear was that it probably meant that I would have to become a missionary in a lonely place. When we become Christians, we talk of having, 'given our lives to Jesus', we make Him the Lord of our lives. It is like saying 'yes' to

Him, before we have seen the plan, and before we know exactly where He will be leading us, so it involves trust.

The wonderful thing about the sacrifice that the Holy Spirit, through Paul, is encouraging is that, unlike the soldiers who die, this is about 'life'. Paul describes how, as we present our bodies to Him as these **living** sacrifices, far from dying, life is going to get richer and better. Two things are involved here:- i) we will stop living according to the pattern we see all around us in the 'world', and ii) we will be transformed as our minds are renewed and we see things God's way. Then we progressively get to see how 'good, pleasing and perfect' His will for us is.

In other words, we are called to sacrifice the 'old me', the one that doesn't please God and will probably mess things up anyway, for the new me 'in Christ'. Giving myself wholly to God is about losing my old self and finding my new self, 'my true child – of – God self'. (John 1:12, The Message). It's a trade in – old for new – that I can't refuse. I'll be letting go of my selfishness and wilfulness – things that often cause me a great deal of trouble anyway – in exchange for His life flowing freely through me. What an invitation!! An invitation to a life of transformation.

I know often times when the Lord has asked me to 'Follow Him', whether in a major life decision, or in a 'nitty gritty' day to day decision, that to say 'yes' to Him has felt hard or sacrificial, and the enemy tries to plant fears in my mind that this is not going to be good for me. If however I can give Him thanks for another opportunity to present myself to Him as a living sacrifice, that will help in the renewing of my mind, and I will begin to see how good His will is for me.

Activation . . .

Thank the Lord always, in those crunch moments. It will align you to His will and remind you again that He is for you and is changing you to be like Jesus. Thanksgiving will help you to accept the invitation to 'offer yourself again as a living sacrifice' – to do life His way, and then your renewed mind will remind you that you are going to get so blessed in the long run, because His will for you is always 'good, pleasing and perfect' **and is always** planned from His heart of love.

DAY 249 | Thanksgiving, Sacrifice and Joy

We finished yesterday's reflection with the thought that thanksgiving will help me to accept the invitation to 'offer myself again as a living sacrifice' – to do life God's way. My renewed mind will remind me that I am going to get so blessed in the long run, because His will for me is always 'good, pleasing and perfect' **and** is planned from His heart of love. So today we are going to look at how being 'a living sacrifice', although often thought of as hard and costly, can be a source of joy,

When we realise that we are called to live sacrificially for the Lord; to 'present our bodies a living and holy sacrifice, acceptable to God, *which is your spiritual service of worship.*' (Romans 12:1, NASB), it can conjure up all sorts of things that we might have to forgo, or that we might have to do that we really would rather not do. It could, and probably will, affect things like our time, our money, or our leisure. It could affect bigger things like where we live, and our choice of career or partner.

It will also affect our day by day relationships, like denying ourselves the right to hold grudges, to gossip, to be angry or to be selfish. The list is really endless, because – yes – offering ourselves as a living sacrifice is going to touch every area of our lives. We will be in agreement with Paul when he writes, 'Do you not know that your body is the temple of the Holy Spirit, who is in you, whom you have received from God? You are not your own; you were bought at a price. Therefore honour God with your body.' (1 Corinthians 6:19, 20). And that would include my tongue, my hands, my feet, my mind and my choices.

"So where is the joy in that?" I hear someone ask. I believe that the joy comes when I see that every call from the Holy Spirit to forego, or to let go of something that I am holding onto, comes out of the heart of the Father who loves me. He sees the things are actually not doing me any good, and the joy comes when I see that letting go of that 'thing' brings me in line with the purposes and plans that God has for me, enabling me to get a great deal closer to the Father. Letting some things go, also frees me up to receive all that He has for me.

Picture the scene – A child is playing with a toy, and is reluctant to give it up or even share it with a sibling or friend. The child holds on tight, strongly defending his/her possession of the toy. Then Dad walks in the room. The child looks up, sees Dad, sees his smile and his open arms of welcome, and so they run and jump into his arms. The toy is forgotten in the light of Dad's presence and the strong arms wrapped around him/her. There is love here, and so joy and laughter are present too.

Paul tells us that giving ourselves as a 'living sacrifice' is our spiritual worship! Now that's a thought too. This is how I worship, not just by singing songs, but by letting go of everything that He wants to take out of my life in order to fully embrace Him, and to receive all He wants to give and pour into my life. This, I believe, is worship in 'spirit and truth (or reality)' (John 4:23), and it brings great joy both to ourselves and God.

David knew about this kind of joy. He writes – and this I believe could be the testimony of any who present their bodies as living sacrifices – 'Lord, you have assigned me my portion and my cup; you have made my lot secure. The boundary lines have fallen for me in pleasant places; surely I have a delightful inheritance ... **I have set the Lord always before me**. Because He is at my right hand I will not be shaken. Therefore my heart is glad and my tongue rejoices; my body also will rest secure, ... You have made known to me the path of life; **you will fill me with joy in your presence, with eternal pleasures at your right hand.**' (Psalm 16:5, 6, 8, 9, 11).

Activation ...

Joy is something that we find in God's presence. He is, after all, the creator and source of all joy. So this is why we can really thank God for every opportunity to follow the Holy Spirit's leading in our lives, even when it feels 'costly'. As you thank Him for each and every opportunity to be 'a living sacrifice', it will remind you that, as you respond to Him, and let go of whatever you are holding onto, you will find yourself (may be a little later) more aware of His presence and full of joy.

This could even begin to make 'dying to (the old) self', a lot of fun!

DAY 250 | Thanksgiving, Presence and Joy!

I have to return to Psalm 16 again this morning. There is more in it for us today, and it really is my most favourite psalm. In the verse with which we finished yesterday, 'You will show me the path of life; in Your presence is fullness of joy, at Your right hand there are pleasures for evermore.' (verse 11, AMP.) The message is simple. David recognises that joy comes as he follows the path in life that the Lord chooses for him, staying close by His side. This is probably the verse that we remember most from this psalm, but it comes on the back of some other very profound declarations.

Written by a king who is also a great military leader, this psalm is a remarkable testament to David's submission to the Lordship of his God. It demonstrates his humility and his dependence on the Lord as well as his trust, love and delight in God. Perhaps all those nights alone on the hillside watching his father's sheep gave him the time that he needed to really get to know God. He had proved that the Lord would help him in his work – protecting the sheep from bears and lions, (1 Samuel 17:34-37), and by the time he comes on the scene, as a young man, commissioned to soothe the King's nerves with his playing, he had also learnt to worship and had become a proficient musician. (1 Samuel 16:23).

At the beginning of the psalm we see how he acknowledges God – not his army – as his true protection, his refuge. Even more than that, he declares that, "... apart from You I have no good", or "no good thing". (Verses 1 & 2). He makes no bones about declaring that he is who he is, and where he is, because that has been the Lord's plan for him, not his own prowess or merit. He says, '**Lord, you** have assigned me my portion and cup . . . The boundary lines have fallen for me in pleasant places; surely I have a delightful inheritance. (Verses 5 & 6).

He also attributes his wisdom to the Lord, speaking of Him as, the one 'who counsels me; even at night my heart instructs me.' And then he explains why he is so confident in the Lord, telling the reader of the intentional choice he has made, 'I have set the Lord always before me. Because he is at my right hand, I will not be shaken.' (Verses 7 & 8).

To me all these statements add up to the fact that David was in harmony with the Lord. There is a sense of his complete 'agreement' with the Lord as he writes this psalm. Now we know that David had his moments when he questioned God, but from this particular psalm, we can just 'feel' the closeness and the friendship that he had with God. It is no wonder that for all his mistakes he was called 'a man after God's own heart', as we see from this psalm how closely he sought to walk with the Lord. As the prophet Amos asks, 'Can two walk together unless they be agreed?' (Amos 3:3 AV).

Out of this place of 'harmony' with God, David could say unequivocally, 'Therefore my heart is glad and my glory [my inner self] rejoices; my body too shall rest *and* confidently dwell in safety.' He has joy in this life and confidence for the next. (Verses 9 & 10. AMP.) And so we reach the concluding verse where David writes of having found such joy in God's presence, and of knowing, with absolute assurance, that at God's right hand, (very close by Him) '*there are* pleasures for evermore.' (Verse 11 AV)

The joy in God that he has comes from walking in harmony and agreement with His God who he knows is for him, with him, and is also planning and preparing the way for him, in all the circumstances of his life. What an amazing revelation that man had, long before Jesus, the cross and the resurrection. He has discovered that saying 'yes' to God's plans and purposes for his life has brought him into a wonderful friendship with the Almighty God; the God who we can now call our Heavenly Father.

So how do we get to walk in this kind of harmony with the Lord; in the kind of agreement with Him that brings us joy? I believe it is by thanking Him and praising Him in all our circumstances. Thanksgiving, as we have seen over the last nine months of reflections, brings us into a place of agreement with God. It helps us to grow in our understanding of His ways. We get to discern His hand in our lives in all the different seasons that we go through. Thanksgiving can even bring us to the place of peace with Him, when we don't understand, enabling us to find that 'fullness of joy in His presence', and the pleasures stored up for us 'at His right hand for evermore'.

Activation . . .

Have a long slow prayerful read of this psalm today, and ask the Holy Spirit to help you to make it your own.

DAY 251 | Thanksgiving, Agreement and Truth

Yesterday we saw (from Psalm 16), how David's agreement with the Lord enabled him to walk very closely with Him. He was therefore able to enjoy the many benefits that that degree of closeness brought him, in body, mind and spirit. Now if agreement with God is so important to our wellbeing, what exactly are we doing when we agree with God? And how we can continue to walk in agreement with God on a daily basis?

In the Song of Moses we have a wonderful description of God, 'He is the Rock, his works are perfect, and all his ways are just. A faithful God who does no wrong, upright and just is he.' (Deuteronomy 32:4). God had previously revealed Himself to Moses as being, 'The Lord, the compassionate and gracious God, slow to anger, abounding in love and faithfulness ...'. (Exodus 34:6). The Psalmist, another man who knew God very well described Him as 'a compassionate and gracious God, slow to anger, abounding in love and faithfulness.' (Psalm 86:15).

In each of those Bible passages the word 'faithful' is translated in the Authorised Version of the Bible as 'Truth', and if we look up the word 'truth' in a concordance, we will see many, many references linking God and 'Truth'. It will soon become clear to any Bible student that God is not just the source of all truth but that He is totally true in all His ways. He is absolutely rock solid faithful to all He says, and to all that He says He will do! Our God is the God of 'truth'. Jesus plainly stated it, declaring, "I am the way and the truth and the life." (John 14:6). John also tells us that, 'grace and truth came through Jesus Christ.' (John 1:17). Furthermore when He was teaching and in His conversations with people Jesus would frequently preface what He said with, "I tell you the truth . . ." No wonder Jesus was very grieved when people didn't believe Him.

On one occasion He even said to the doubting Jews, "Yet because I tell you the truth, you do not believe me . . . He who belongs to God hears what God says. The reason you do not hear is that you do not belong to God." (John 8:45-47). Serious words indeed, and somewhat offensive because He had already told them that they were unable to hear Him because they belonged to their father – the devil, of whom Jesus said, "there is no truth in him. When he lies, he speaks his native language, for he is a liar and the father of lies."(John 8:43,44). God speaks the truth and the devil speaks lies. We can all agree with this I am sure. How is it then that many of us find it easier, on occasion, to believe the devil's lies than to believe God's truth? Maybe you're not sure about that. Well ask yourself, 'How often have I doubted that God really loves me, that He actually delights in me, that Christ is in me, and that nothing can separate me from His love?

When you pay someone a compliment and they say something like, "well it's kind of you to say that, **but** ...", we feel a bit shut out. The person is basically saying, "You are not really telling me the truth." How much nicer is it when, after we have given someone a compliment they say, "Thank you, I receive that", and we see them absorb our words and grow stronger in some way because of them? Well this is how the Lord feels about the things He says to us in His word. He is never going to be speaking lies, or saying things to us just to flatter us or make us feel OK. And this is why we need to agree with God when he speaks to us through His word as we read His truths about us – His 'New Creation'. (2 Corinthians 5:17).

Agreement with God, from deep down in our being, exposes and deals with any doubt and unbelief, because when we try and confess a truth out loud and it 'sticks in the throat', we know that we have not fully received that truth. When we find ourselves effectively saying to God, "Well thank you God, but really I know you are just being nice to me, or just encouraging me", we are in fact disagreeing with God, and believing the lies of the enemy. And that is the exact opposite of faith.

'God is not a man that He should lie,' (Numbers 23:19). He is in fact 'God who cannot lie,' (Titus 1:2, NASB), so agreeing with God enables me to walk in harmony with Him because, as I agree with Him, my faith levels rise and we know that God loves faith. He loves to see faith in our hearts more than anything else because without it we can't please Him. (Hebrews 11:6).

Activation ...

Thank the Lord today that He is totally true in all His dealings with you, and that He only ever speaks truth into your heart, never half truths and certainly never lies.

DAY 252 | Thanksgiving, Agreement and Faith

So yesterday we established that our God is a God of truth. Unlike any human being, and clearly unlike the devil, He only, ever speaks truth into our lives. It is also true that accepting and believing what He says to us, and about us, is our main source of faith because 'Faith comes from hearing, and hearing by the word of Christ.' (Romans 10:17, NASB.) Jesus Himself said to the enemy, "Man does not live on bread alone, but on every word that comes from the mouth of God". (Matthew 4:4). What God says to us is truth and also spiritual 'life' itself.

Jesus often challenged His listeners saying, "He who has ears to hear, let Him hear." (Luke 8:8). Now clearly the vast majority of His listeners had ears, but Jesus was talking about really hearing Him and embracing what He was saying. Really 'hearing' God is a question of the heart and we know, because Jesus said it, that 'out of the overflow of the heart the mouth speaks.' (Matthew 12:34). What we hear and believe will sooner or later be expressed through our mouths.

We read that, 'Death and life are in the power of the tongue.' (Proverbs 18:21, NASB). Well since we are not kings and queens to say, 'Off with her/his head", we know that we don't literally have the power to command life or death for someone, but we do have the power in our tongues to give or take away 'life' from ourselves, because the confessions of my mouth, coming from my heart agreement with what I have heard from God, and from His word, are vital for my spiritual life.

Now some of the truths that we read in the Bible are really hard to believe, when we look at our own life, or measure 'how we are doing'. But thanking God for His words and His truth can help to bring us into agreement and therefore alignment with God, and that close walk with Him. Then the confessions that we hear coming from our own mouths start to erode that unbelief and, with the Holy Spirit's help, they build our faith.

As we move forward towards the goal of complete agreement with God, the walls of unbelief and fear will come down; there will be nothing between us, and like David we will find that, "Because he is at my right hand I will not be shaken." (Psalm 16:8). This closeness then brings with it the joy and pleasure that there is to be found in His presence.

There are just so many words that we need to agree with, words that can transform our lives, and for those of you who are saying, "Ah yes but surely that was said to the nation of Israel, or that was God speaking to Paul, or the early Christian community", let us remember what we wrote on a previous day, that what the Lord has spoken to anyone of His beloved children we can say, as His well loved child, "and me too please!" In other words we need to, and can, appropriate and claim all of God's words for ourselves.

Activation . . .

'The words of the Lord are flawless, like silver refined in a furnace of clay, purified seven times.' (Psalm 12:6), so today let us take a truth that we are finding hard to believe; a scripture where we are in a certain level of disagreement with God. (It's called unbelief!) Let us look at something about His love, His purposes and good plans for us, or His care of us, and then let us find the 'truth' in scripture and thank God for it until we believe it. We all have our challenging areas, so here are a few 'starters', or you can find your own:-

'I have loved you with an everlasting love'. (Jeremiah 31:3).

'As far as the east is from the west, so far has he removed our transgressions from us.' (Psalm 103:12).

'The lord your God is with you, he is mighty to save. He will take great delight in you . . . He will rejoice over you with singing.' (Zephaniah 3:17).

"For I know the plans I have for you . . . plans to prosper you and not to harm you, plans to give you hope and a future." (Jeremiah 29:11).

'My times are in your hands'. (Psalm 31:15).

'Christ in you, the hope of glory.' (Colossians 1:27).

'And we know that in all things God works for the good of those who love Him, who have been called according to his purpose.' (Romans 8:28).

'Here I am! I stand at the door and knock. If anyone hears my voice and opens the door, I will come in and eat with him and he with me.' (Revelation 3:20).

DAY 253 | Thanksgiving, Truth and revival

The word 'revive' literally means to come back to conscious existence or to life, vivre being the Latin for life. Yesterday we quoted Proverbs 18:21 that, 'Death and life are in the power of the tongue'. What we speak has the power to bring us life or death... Sounds a bit dramatic, but not if we truly believe that we live by every word that proceeds from the mouth of the Father, because His words are 'TRUTH' through and through.

We sometimes talk about meditating or 'feeding' on the word of God. Meditating has the same meaning as ruminating, i.e. chewing over and over, as a cow does the cud; it therefore carries the idea of getting all the nourishment for life from it. The Lord says to us through Psalm 81:10, 'Open wide your mouth and I will fill it.' or from The Passion Translation we read, 'Open your mouth now with a mighty decree and I will fill it.'

The psalm continues, 'If my people would but listen to me... how quickly I would subdue their enemies and turn my hand against their foes!... But you would be fed with the finest of wheat; with honey from the rock I would satisfy you." From the Passion Translation this reads, 'But my people wouldn't listen;... O that my people would once and for all listen to me and walk faithfully in my footsteps, following in my ways, Then and only then will I conquer your every foe, telling them "You must go!" "But I will feed you with my spiritual bread. You will feast and be satisfied with me, feeding on my revelation truth like honey dripping from the cliffs of the high places." (Psalm 81:10,11,16, TPT.)

In the Book of Revelation 12:10 & 11 we read of those saints who overcame the devil – who accuses God's people before God day and night – by 'the blood of the Lamb and the word of their testimony.' That is to say, they agreed with and spoke out in faith that Jesus death and resurrection was the basis of their being able to come before God. They declared to the devil exactly what Jesus has done for them through the shedding of His blood on the cross.

Smith Wigglesworth, who lived and saw the Lord do amazing things by the power of the Holy Spirit, spells out for us his belief in the power of agreeing with what God says and speaking it out; declaring it! He believed that listening, hearing what God says and declaring it, agreeing with it and speaking it out, is the key to personal revival, Spirit and Word operating together. We all therefore have the power to give ourselves a life giving boost through speaking out over ourselves these vital truths that God has spoken.

One time when Paul was feeling very depleted by 'a messenger of Satan' the Lord says to him in response to his prayers for deliverance, 'My grace is sufficient for you, for my power is made perfect in weakness.' Paul embraces this 'word' from God with such wholehearted agreement that he can declare, 'Therefore I will boast all the more gladly about my weaknesses, so that Christ's power May rest on me . . . For when I am weak, then I am strong.' (2 Corinthians 12:9,10). We have a sword with which we can defeat our enemy when he has, or is threatening to, overrun us. Interestingly it is called the sword of the Spirit and it is the word of God. (Ephesians 6:17). God's words, as we take hold of them and declare them out loud, become our sword with which we fight off enemy attack. How wonderful is that? Death and Life are in the power of the tongue, and we can all do this!!

Activation . . .

Next time you feel accused, condemned by the devil, remember to 'overcome' his accusations by remembering and declaring out loud that you are cleansed by the blood of the Lamb and that there is therefore now 'no condemnation for those who are in Christ Jesus, because through Christ Jesus the law of the Spirit of life set me free from the law of sin and death.' (Romans 8:1, 2). 'For you know that it was not with perishable things such as silver and gold that you were redeemed from the empty way of life that was handed down to you from your forefathers, but with the precious blood of the Christ, a lamb without blemish or defect.' (1 Peter 1:18). And when feeling oppressed, declare that, 'in all these things we are more than conquerors through him who loved us.' (Romans 8:37-39).

DAY 254 | Thanksgiving that God's Words carry His Power

When God speaks things happen. In the very first book of the Bible at the start of our world, the phrase, 'And God said' occurs nine times, (Genesis 1:3,6,9,11,14,20,24,26,29), and when 'God said', amazing things happened. Jesus Himself is the radiance of the Father's glory, and the exact representation of His being sustaining all things by His powerful word'. (Hebrews 1:3). So God's words created and now sustain everything that we see all around us.

Jesus Himself is called 'the Word'. (John 1:1). God has spoken and revealed Himself through Jesus and we read in the Gospels of the amazing things that happened when Jesus used His words to speak to people and into situations while He was on earth. Jesus, sending a report to John the Baptist, says of the effect of His words that 'The blind receive sight, the lame walk, those who have leprosy are cured, the deaf hear, the dead are raised and good news is preached to the poor'. (Matthew 11:5). Miracles and healings happen when Jesus speaks.

This is why when we hear God's word spoken into our lives we can expect things to happen. We can expect change to come as we actively 'hear' and believe, or 'agree' with His words. As we take hold of God's words we should feel a sense of excitement and anticipation because, 'the word of God is living and active.' (Hebrews 4:12). Since God only speaks 'truth', we need to give thanks to Him for every word that He speaks, because God's word can be an instrument of change in our lives, making us more like Christ, and so more able to represent Him to our world.

God's written Word refines us as we read it, hear it, and chew it over, (meditate on it). It is 'Sharper than any double edged sword, it penetrates even to the dividing of soul and spirit, joints and marrow; it judges the thoughts and attitudes of the heart.' (Hebrews 4:12). This is why embracing God's Word is a big part of personal revival. If we will let it, it will help us to sort out our motivations and those deep seated attitudes that can be harmful to us and to others. Just as God's word was powerful to create Light and Life out of darkness and emptiness (Genesis 1 and Hebrews 1:3) so His word is still powerful to work this healing, transforming, creative work in our lives, changing us to be more like Jesus, day by day.

Psalm 119:9-11, reminds us that God's word can also help us to avoid sin, 'I have hidden your word in my heart, that I might not sin against you'. It can also bring correction to our lives and direction. Psalm 119:105 says 'Your word is a lamp to my feet and a light for my path' and later in verse 129 & 130 the psalmist says, 'Your statutes are wonderful; therefore I obey them. The unfolding of your words gives light; it gives understanding to the simple.'

Let us today gratefully thank the Lord for His written word, and for the truths that He has provided for us to feed on. And as we thankfully welcome those words into our lives, the Holy Spirit will take those words and renew our minds. (Romans 12:2). We will be transformed by the power of the word and the Spirit working in us, because God has said 'My word that goes out from my mouth will not return to me empty but will accomplish what I desire and achieve the purpose for which I sent it'. (Isaiah 55:11).

Activation . . .

Jesus was able to say categorically to the devil, 'Man does not live on bread alone, but on every word that comes from the mouth of God.' (Matthew 4:4). Let us be so thankful that we have a speaking God, who declares who He is, what He loves, and how He wants us to live. He has spoken through creation, through His word and through Jesus. He has not left us to guess who He is or what He is like. So receive with gladness everything that He reveals to you about Himself so that you might 'know' and love Him with all your heart, mind, soul and strength.

Give thanks too for every transformative word that He 'speaks' into your spirit. Welcome His 'Words' with all their healing and restorative power, with your thanksgiving, and see how they bring life giving peace and joy into your heart and mind.

DAY 255 | The Fulfillment of Prophesy

Yesterday we were considering the power that is released into our lives, as God speaks. When God speaks His words can also bring change to our circumstances. Remember how the centurion said to Jesus, ". . . just say the word and my servant will be healed." (Matthew 8:8). In the Old Testament we have an amazing promise from God about His words. Speaking to the Israelites He said, "As the rain and the snow come down from heaven, and do not return to it without watering the earth and making it bud and flourish, so that it yields seeds for the sower and bread for the eater, so is my word that goes out from my mouth: It will not return to me empty, but will accomplish what I desire and achieve the purpose for which I sent it." (Isaiah 55:10,11).

Now we know that as well as speaking to us through scripture God speaks to us prophetically by His Spirit through the gifts that He freely gives. In these days, when there is an increase of God speaking 'prophetically' through his body, (and remember we can 'all prophesy', see 1 Corinthians 14:31), we clearly need to be able to discern that the words that we hear through each other, or directly for ourselves, truly are from God. And so Paul encourages us to 'weigh carefully what is said.' (1 Corinthians 14:29).

If we do want to give someone a 'word' or when we receive a 'word' from someone else, our first means of 'weighing it' is through the scriptures. This is because we know that the Holy Spirit is the Spirit of truth and so no word 'inspired by the Holy Spirit' is going to contradict the scriptures. Secondly we should also be able to sense within our own spirit a measure of agreement with what is said to us, and finally we should always share those 'words' with others who we trust, so that they can add their understanding, clarification, and verification of what God is saying as described in 1 Corinthians 14:29.

The wonder of hearing from God through a prophetic word or picture, a word of knowledge, or a word of wisdom, is that faith rises in our hearts because it feels like God has seen us, seen our situation and heard our hearts cry, and then spoken to us personally. This is especially so if the person bringing that 'word' does not know our circumstances. It is not hard in those situations, when we have an immediate 'witness' in our spirit that these words are from God, to rejoice and be thankful. Giving thanks for any 'prophetic words' that we receive can also be a way of testing those words because it will ensure that our spirit and Holy Spirit will be in harmony.

Thanksgiving for a prophetic word is also important in making it 'active' and effective in our lives. This is because prophetic words are not the same as fortune telling! That is to say they don't carry a 'prediction' or a fatalistic message. When God speaks a word to us, through scripture, or through another Christian, we need to keep revisiting those words and talking to God about them. As we hold those words before the Lord, with gratitude in our hearts, we can know that He says, "I am watching to see that my word is fulfilled." (Jeremiah 1:12). Our faith will then grow. Delay won't deplete it. This is so important because the fulfillment of God's word is not always instant; His timings are so very often different to ours, and fulfillment may well require patience and perseverance, as it did for Abraham.

As we wait on the Lord our thanksgiving will not only sustain and increase our faith, it will also help us to grow our understanding of what God is saying, thereby helping to keep us from presumption about how those words might be fulfilled. Thanksgiving and ruminating over the words that God has spoken to us will enable us to take on board at a deeper level all that the Lord is saying, and give room for the Holy Spirit to guide us if there are conditions that we ourselves need to fulfill. If God is speaking, the Holy Spirit is definitely involved, and will be instrumental in the fulfillment of that word; our part is to give thanks and praise and to walk with the Lord, building our faith and understanding as we go.

Activation . . .

Remind yourself of, and revisit those 'words' that the Lord has spoken to you from the scriptures or through another Christian, and intentionally give thanks for those 'words', remembering that it is through, 'faith and patience that we inherit what has been promised.' (Hebrews 6:12). Like Abraham be fully persuaded that, 'what he had promised, he was able also to perform.' (Romans 4:21. AV). 'Blessed is she that believe; there shall be a performance of those things that were told her from the Lord.' (Luke 1:45. AV).

DAY 256 | Thanksgiving and Reason

We have been reflecting recently on the fact that God is a God of truth, that He always speaks the truth and that His words of truth are a sure foundation for our faith and life. In our post modern world however, we find ourselves in an age where the concepts of 'my truth' and, 'how I feel', get to be more important than absolute truth, objective facts, or even investigation to find the truth. In the church too, experience and feelings have sometimes been elevated above God's objective truth in His Word, the Bible, and so 'reason' and 'thinking' may also suffer a bad press.

If we add to this the things that we have considered previously concerning the apparent contradictions, and perplexities that we encounter in the life of faith as we walk with God, it can sometimes feels very confusing when it comes to understanding what is going on and where God is for us in a particular situation. Maybe you have had the experience of someone saying, "Don't try and think it through, or reason this out. Just have faith." And that can feel a bit trite and superficial, or maybe it's just too hard to discount your thoughts and feelings in a situation, and so your faith in God and walk with Him takes a knock.

Since the reformation and renaissance, up until recently, we have lived in a time when reason, logic and scientific thought were paramount. Culture now seems to be changing. So is reason no longer an important ingredient when it comes to staying in faith in God's truth when our feelings and circumstances are adverse? Well today I want to delve into a very interesting passage in the chapter of Faith – Hebrews 11:17-19, the story of Abraham and his faith in offering Isaac. Isaac, remember, was to be the fulfillment of God's promises to Abraham that he would father first of all a son, and then a nation. The passage is written to demonstrate his great faith, but what do we read in verse 19? 'Abraham reasoned (reckoned or considered) that God could raise the dead, ...'. Wow! That sounds like Abraham was thinking and reasoning when he acted in faith by obeying God and in being willing to sacrifice his son, his promise of an incredible inheritance.

So faith can be fed by thinking and reasoning. Perhaps this is why Romans 12:2 talks about the importance of our thinking, reasoning apparatus, our minds, being renewed. Now using our reasoning skills is not always the same as understanding. We can be in a place of not understanding why certain hard things are happening, but we can still harness our reason to the truths about God, about His ways, His promises, and His commitment to us, so that we nourish and grow our faith and act accordingly. Abraham may well have not understood 'why' God was asking him to sacrifice Isaac, or 'how' God's request fitted in with his understanding of God, His character and ways, and His promise, but he was ready to proceed.

So how does thanksgiving fit in with all this? Well we have already looked at how thanksgiving is a magnificently practical way of building our faith; at how every time we thank God for His goodness, love, faithfulness and more, we are not just blessing God, we are rehearsing the truth to ourselves; we are reminding our brain and our thoughts that these are the facts about God, and so, illuminated by the Holy Spirit, we are renewing our minds. If Abraham had been continually thanking God and reminding himself that God was unerringly good and always kept His promises, his thinking would be strongly renewed and predicated along those lines. So then when he got to the top of the mountain with Isaac it would be quite reasonable to have faith in the God of the resurrection. (Hebrews 11:19)

Activation . . .

Let thanksgiving inform your mind, brain and reasoning powers with truth. Unleash your thanksgiving, your declaration of God's truth, and let it thereby renew your mind and feed your faith. The more you do this the more reasonable faith becomes, even at times when you may not understand everything that God is doing. Learn to reason with a renewed mind and let the Holy Spirit come together with your thanksgiving to feed your faith and your trust in your wonderful Lord.

DAY 257 | Thanksgiving and Evaluating what is Important

Yesterday we reflected on how using our reason based on God's truth, combined with the Holy Spirit's wisdom, and a heart of thanksgiving can build, grow and strengthen our faith. We saw how Abraham, our Father of Faith (Romans 4:16), used his mind and reasoning to feed his faith, and we remembered how thanksgiving is a key way to feed our minds with truth about God and His promises. Thanksgiving is therefore not a trite, or superficial, alternative to thought and reason as some might have claimed.

Today let's go back again to Hebrews 11 and read about someone else who used his brain and reason to help himself grow in faith, make good choices, and fulfill his destiny; something we might all like to do! Moses is that man, and in Hebrews 11:24-26 we read that Moses chose to go God's way by refusing to go on with a golden, privileged, pleasure filled life as Pharaoh's grandson. It was a 'hard' choice because clearly he had to refuse the multiple benefits of privilege, and embrace mistreatment and disgrace as a result. Verse 24 makes it clear that he did this by faith.

This was not mindless faith, blind optimism, or thoughtless belief that "it will all be alright" like in some Hollywood films. Look hard at verse 26. It talks about, 'esteeming' (AV) or 'considering' (NASB/AMP) or 'regarding' the reproach of Christ greater riches, (NASB), 'greater value' (NIV), 'greater wealth' (AMP) than the treasures of Egypt. I would like to suggest that Moses over time 'considered', that is to say he thought long and hard about it all. Now I am sure his spirit and his faith were to the fore in this process, but his brain and reason were involved too. Much later we can see, from the discussions he had with God at the burning bush, that his emotions and initial thoughts about going back to Egypt were not happy ones and he needed some persuasion. (Exodus Chapters 3 and 4).

I love pictures and allegories. Could Moses have read a heavenly 'Which' magazine at this point? Shall I choose the flashy 4x4 with all the bells, whistles and comforts, but which the report says will break down after five years and is hopeless off road? Or shall I go for the more expensive, 'land rover' type that will cost me all my savings. It's a bit old fashioned, with fewer creature comforts, less 'street cred.', but it's utterly reliable, goes everywhere with me and will last forever? Which one will be more valuable in the long term? Do you think that Moses read the heavenly 'Which' reviews of the relative merits of following God by faith through difficulty and reproach, against the flashy, enjoyable but temporary, pleasures of Egypt? All of his spirit, reason and emotions are in play here. Then having considered it carefully, and done a full evaluation and assessment, he made a faith decision on what was more valuable because, we are told, 'he was looking ahead to his reward...' (Hebrews 11:26).

I hear echoes here of the parables Jesus told about the man who found a pearl of great price and valued it so highly that he sold everything to buy it. Also the man who found hidden treasure in a field that he valued so highly that it was worth selling everything he had to buy that field. (Matthew 13:44-46). Both parables speak strongly of the importance of the process of evaluating things in my heart, mind and spirit. And of course faith is all interwoven in that because it is by faith that they, like Moses, made their true evaluation of the worth of Christ and of following Him.

And thanksgiving? Well they say 'beauty is in the eye of the beholder'. So I suggest that the more I gaze on Jesus and remind myself with frequent gratitude and thanksgiving of all He means to me and all He has done for me and continues to do for me, the more my true evaluation of His preciousness to me will increase. The same will be true as I thank and adore my loving Heavenly Father, and appreciate my beautiful helper the Holy Spirit.

Activation...

Today let your thanksgiving feed your assessment of the value of having given your life to Jesus. Let your thanksgiving enable you to see that anything you have had to sacrifice, or will sacrifice, to stay close to Jesus is not even worth a second glance. Above all else, grow to be like Paul who wrote, 'For me to live is Christ and to die is gain.' (Phil 1:21) and, 'I want to know Christ and the power of his resurrection...,' and 'I press on to take hold of that which Christ Jesus took hold of me.' (Phil 3:10, 12).

DAY 258 | Thanksgiving and 'Reckoning'

It's that wonderful word 'reckon' that I want to focus on today. It's another word that indicates that it's very ok to use our minds, our reasoning and our thinking on this life journey of 'faith'. It's also one of the most intriguing exhortations in the bible. Paul uses that word 'reckon' in his letter to the Romans writing, **'reckon (count) yourselves dead to sin, but alive to God in Christ Jesus.'** (Romans 6:11). The context is that Paul, after expounding the wonders of limitless grace, tackles the problem of those who might say, "Well OK then it doesn't matter if I sin, I can do what I like, because there will always be more forgiveness available." Paul's counter argument goes like this...

'Or don't you know that all of us who were baptised into Christ Jesus were baptised into His death? We were therefore buried with Him through baptism into death in order that, just as Christ was raised from the dead through the glory of the Father, we too may live a new life. If we have been united with Him like this in His death, we will certainly also be united with Him in His resurrection. For we know that our old self was crucified with Him so that the body of sin might be done away with, that we should no longer be slaves to sin – because anyone who has died has been freed from sin. Now if we died with Christ, we believe that we will also live with Him ... The death he died, he died to sin once for all, but the life He lives he lives to God. (Romans 6:1-10).

I don't think many of us would fall into the category of those, who think that grace means that I can now do whatever I like because forgiveness will follow, but Paul's exhortation to 'reckon yourself dead to sin' certainly applies to those of us who are trying to subdue the 'old me' in order to live a Godly life. Christians who want to follow the Lord, by obeying and honouring Him in all they do, are often plagued by the enemy's accusations as he shows us our failures and where we need to do better. We've all been there, and if we are not careful this can push us into just 'trying harder'. We can end up 'trying' to stop what is not good in our thoughts and behaviours, and then 'trying' to do better. This can all be very hard work!

The enemy's tactic is simply to keep our focus on our mistakes, sins and shortcomings. What I did or didn't do that I should have done, or could have done. What I thought or said that I shouldn't have etc. It's not hard for him to do that, and sometimes the more we try to compensate and make up for these things the harder it gets. This is because whatever takes our focus, and fills our mind and spirit, will be magnified. We are in fact 'looking' at the wrong thing and so we keep ourselves living out of the 'old me' mentality.

If instead, like Paul, we declare by faith, 'I have been crucified with Christ, and I no longer live, but Christ lives in me. The life I live in the body, I live by faith in the Son of God, who loved me and gave Himself for me.' (Galatians 2:20), followed by, "Thank you Lord for the grace to live out of my new life in Christ in this situation", it all gets a lot easier. By turning to Him with thanksgiving I am simply lifting my thoughts again to the true facts of the situation. Thanksgiving for 'my new life in Christ' enables me to 'reckon' on the 'New Life' and all the grace pouring into me.

When we 'reckon' on something being right or true, we act accordingly. So if I 'reckon' that my employer or pension provider has transferred some money into my account, I will feel free to go and spend it, and I most certainly won't try and earn that money all over again, because it is now legally mine. Likewise if I reckon that I am now 'dead to sin, but alive to God in Christ Jesus', I will also reckon that His life within will be empowering me to 'walk as Jesus did,' (1 John 2: 6). Focusing and reckoning on 'My new life in Christ', releases the faith in me that allows that new life to grow stronger and stronger.

Activation . . .

What a wonderfully liberating truth this is. It's the truth that becoming a Christian is not a patch up job on the old me, but a whole new way of living empowered by the Holy Spirit. Today let's say, "Thank you Lord so much, this is indeed almost too good to be true!!" Then if or when you are tempted to sin or you fail God in some way, let your thanksgiving shift your default setting from, 'Must try harder' to, 'Thank you Lord for the grace to live out my new life in Christ in this situation'. In this way let the Holy Spirit help you to 'reckon' on His life in you, and the grace that is available to you.

Refuse all 'Must do better' thoughts with thanksgiving for God's love, forgiveness, and your **new life in Christ**. 'Reckon' on that flow of grace, knowing it can't be earned, nor is any kind of penance required.

DAY 259 | Thanksgiving that I am a New Creation

Yesterday we were looking at the indwelling power that is ours when we 'reckon ourselves dead to sin but alive to God in Christ Jesus.' (Romans 6:11). It's the power to live life from the Christ life within, and to 'walk as He walked.' (1 John 2:6). So here, at the heart of our Christian life, is the enormous mystery that, '... if anyone is in Christ he is a new creation; the old has gone, the new has come!' (2 Corinthians 5:17).

We said yesterday that becoming a Christian is not a patch up job for the 'old me', but a whole new way of living powered by the Holy Spirit. Grasping this mind blowing mystery is a challenge to us all, but if we can, it is a key to entering that 'rest of faith' about which the writer to the Hebrews talks. 'There remains, then, a Sabbath-rest for the people of God; for anyone who enters God's rest also rests from his own work, just as God did from his'. (Hebrews 4:9, 10).

'Being redeemed' means that when I was born again Jesus took my old man to the cross and gave me His life in exchange. If I have been crucified with Christ, then His life in me carries His spiritual DNA, and now **all** I have the do is choose to let his life flow out in my thoughts, words and deeds. I say **all**, because as we know our old ways of being and doing linger on, and this is why I need to have my mind renewed because my mind can still think as the 'old me'. And so the whole process of sanctification – becoming like Jesus – is about learning to live from the 'new me' within by, 'reckoning' that my old self has died with Christ and that now Christ lives in me and (if I'll let Him) through me.

Paul conveys in several of his letters that there is always a choice involved in this process. He writes, don't do the old stuff but, '... clothe yourself with the Lord Jesus Christ, and do not think about how to gratify the desires of the sinful nature.' (Romans 13:14). '... for all of you who were baptised into Christ have clothed yourself with Christ.' (Galatians 3:27), 'Do not lie to each other, since you have taken off your old self with its practices and have put on the new self, which is being renewed in knowledge in the image of its Creator.' (Colossians 3:9, 10). And to the Ephesians he writes, 'You were taught, with regard to your former way of life, to put off your old self, which is being corrupted by its deceitful desires; to be made new in the attitude of your minds; and to put on the new self, created to be like God in true righteousness and holiness.' (Ephesians 4:22 – 24).

It seems to me that putting off the old and living from the new has a lot to do with how we are thinking and therefore the choices that we are making. This then is, once again, where the powerful weapon of thanksgiving comes to our aid. The more that I can thank the Lord that 'I am a new creation', that 'the old has gone and the new has come', the more my faith will grow in who I now am 'in Christ'. I will be more alert and in tune to how my new nature, guided and empowered by the Holy Spirit, wants to behave. Thanksgiving that I have a new nature and a new life in Christ deep within will enable me, in any situation, to recognise when the habits of the 'old me' are trying to get resurrected. 'Putting off the old' becomes a choice because I am not going to battle the old, I am just going to remember and 'reckon' on the fact that it has been replaced with the new.

How does this work? Well let's take a simple example.

I find myself getting exasperated by a situation. I am getting fretful and agitated, so I begin to say, "Thank you Jesus, that I am a new creation and that I have your life within. I thank you for the Holy Spirit who is producing in me the beautiful fruit of patience through this situation. I turn away from agitation, and choose again to let your life flow in and through me. I thank you that from Your life within can come the wisdom to know what to do here, and in fact You and I together can walk through this time in peace, and even with some joy and laughter."

Activation . . .

Have a go!! Thanksgiving can truly make being sanctified fun.

DAY 260 | Thanksgiving and My New Life Within

One of the things that is quite amazing about our salvation, is this ongoing revelation that this is not just about what happens when I die, but also about the fact that I now already have Christ's life within. The Apostle Peter puts it like this, 'His divine power has given us everything we need for life and godliness, through our knowledge of him who called us by his own glory and goodness. Through these he has given us his very great and precious promises, so that through them you may participate in the divine nature and escape the corruption that is in the world caused by evil.' (2 Peter 1:3,4).

Note that he uses the past tense and reminds us several times that certain things **have already been given** to us so that we can **now 'participate' or share in God's divine nature**. Incredible or what? You and I have, as we take hold of those promises, been granted everything pertaining to life and godliness. Everything we need to live from the Christ life within. We are not just a 'New Creation' like a shiny new casserole dish purchased empty, but ready for use, we are that 'dish' already filled with all that we need to produce a delicious meal. These scriptures explain to us that we are already in receipt of, and being increasingly filled with, that 'new life'

This resonates with the encouragement quoted yesterday from the writings of the apostle Paul, encouraging us to 'reckon (count) yourselves dead to sin, but alive to God in Christ Jesus. We wrote that focusing and reckoning on 'My new life in Christ', releases the faith in me that allows that new life to grow stronger and stronger. Sometimes, however, it's hard to believe that there really is a new life within.

I can believe that 'I am a new creation', but perhaps find it harder to believe that 'the old has gone, the new has come.' (2 Corinthians 5:17). It really is an incredible truth but one that it is so important for us to fully grasp and believe, if we are going to live out of that new life, and not try to reform the old. The challenge now is to believe and so let ourselves 'Be filled with all the measure of the fullness of God.' (Ephesians 3:19).

A spin off of recognising that it is all about believing these amazing promises and receiving the power that they carry, is that it causes me to 'walk humbly with my God.' (Micah 6:8). Once I grasp that, like forgiveness and new birth, living from the 'new me', the Christ life within, is all about grace and not self effort or merit, then there is then no room for self congratulatory thoughts but all the glory does indeed go to Jesus. This is because I know without a shadow of doubt that it is only the power of the Holy Spirit that enables me to live as this new creation in Christ.

Graham Cooke explains it like this, 'It's not about your effort or struggle to be better. We are asking you to focus on His life and to learn to walk in Him, through Him, as Him, and with Him. *His life, righteousness, holiness, grace, faith, character and power all belong to you*'.[1] The common clay pot about which Paul speaks in Corinthians does not try to become 'the treasure within', rather the treasure is 'put' there for the pot to carry. 2 Corinthians 4:7).

Activation . . .

'There is a divine mystery – a secret surprise that has been concealed from the world for generations, but now it's being revealed, unfolded and manifested for every holy believer to experience. Living within you is the Christ who floods you with the expectation of glory! This mystery of Christ embedded within us, becomes a heavenly treasure chest of hope filled with the riches of glory for his people, and God wants everyone to know it.' (Colossians 1:26, 27 TPT).

So now we truly have just one more reason to be thankful because, as we continue to gives thanks for this amazing aspect of our salvation, we will see just how incredible it all is and join with Paul in saying, *'to the only wise God be glory for ever through Jesus Christ! Amen.'* (Romans 16:27).

DAY 261 | Thanksgiving for things "Beyond Belief"

I wonder if like me you find the mystery of the 'indwelling Christ' almost too amazing to fully grasp. Sometimes I feel like the psalmist when he writes, 'When I consider your heavens and the work of your fingers, the moon and the stars, which you have set in place, what is man that you are mindful of him, the son of man that you care for him?' (Psalm 8:4). Creation is just so amazing and so awesome, so complex and wonderful, it does indeed seem incredible that God should be mindful of me, and more than that, actually care for me, answer my prayers and place the Christ life in me, thus allowing me to carry His glory in this world. (John 17:20-23).

In the face of all that we now know about the wonders of creation, I can still feel that measure of it all being beyond belief that God would come and dwell with and in me for my whole life. One time when I was expressing this to the Lord, worrying that this was really just unbelief, I felt that the Lord was saying, "This is not 'unbelief', it's incredulity and it's O.K to be incredulous, because I can help you with that." So what is the difference between incredulity and unbelief? Well not a great deal, according to the dictionary, but I think it is actually a thing of the heart.

The incredulous man maybe wants to believe, like the boy's Father who said, "Lord I do believe, help me overcome my unbelief." (Mark 9:24). He believed that Jesus **could** heal his boy, but was finding it hard to believe that Jesus **would**. This was very different to the Pharisees who were aggressively unbelieving. They were trying to goad Jesus into 'performing' for them. They were not really wanting His help, just wanting to catch Him out and expose Him to ridicule. (Matthew 12:38,39).

It may be because of Jesus response to those particular leaders, which was, "A wicked and adulterous generation asks for a miraculous sign! But none shall be given . . .", that we are sometimes told that we shouldn't ask for a sign, as it shows a lack of faith and trust; but what about Gideon? Gideon didn't doubt that God existed. He'd had an amazing encounter with the Lord.

As a result he had cut down His Father's Asherah pole and rallied the men in order to fight the Midianites and Amalekites. (Judges 6:25-28,34,35).

In the following verses (36-40) Gideon asks twice for the, now famous, 'fleece' signs. Gideon didn't need God to give him a sign to show him that He could defeat all these armies, but he was incredulous that it could be, "by my hand, as you said." He was incredulous that the victory would come through his leading of the army of Manasseh, Asher, Zebulun and Naphtali. So God gave Him two signs and didn't tell him off! Then recognizing that Gideon still needed reassurance God spontaneously gave him a third sign, Judges 7:9-15. How kind is that?

In a different way Mary who, in spite of having had an angel tell her that she would have a baby, asks a practical question. "How can this be . . .?" She is then told about the Holy Spirit's involvement and she is also given a 'sign'. 'Your relative Elizabeth has also conceived a son in her old age . . .' Luke 2:26-38). Both Gideon and Mary did not doubt that God was present and active, but in different ways had questions about how the incredible things spoken of could happen. They could be said to be incredulous, not unbelieving. Sometimes we can think, 'Well if I saw an angel all my doubts would vanish and I would do and believe whatever the Lord said', but maybe our incredulity would still manifest itself in some way.

Activation . . .

I believe therefore that if we can keep our heart full of thanksgiving for all that the Lord has said and done for us in the past, we will more than likely be full of faith and less incredulous when He speaks to us prophetically, like He did to Gideon, or when we ask Him to intervene, like the sick boy's Father. A heart full of thanksgiving will also help us to hear those encouragements and confirmatory 'signs', that the Lord is willing to give. Then, rather than saying to Him "How can this happen?" we will respond with "Thank you Lord, I do believe that you are living in me, but now please increase my faith."

DAY 262 | Thanksgiving and Transformation

God's plan for us in giving us our 'new Christ life' is that we should grow and be changed. 'But we all, with unveiled face, beholding as in a mirror the glory of the Lord, are being transformed into the same image from glory to glory, just as from the Lord the Spirit.' (2 Corinthians 3:18, NASB), or as it is written in the Amplified Bible, we are being changed 'from one degree of glory to another'.

We have a God who is always increasing His power and His glory on the earth. 'Of the increase of His government and peace there will be no end.' (Isaiah 9:7), and ultimately, '... the earth will be filled with the knowledge of the glory of the Lord, as the waters cover the sea.' (Habakkuk 2:14). We are a very significant part of this great plan and so His intention is always to find ways of increasing His glory in our lives too.

His plan for you and me is that we being 'rooted deep in love and founded securely on love, ... may have the power be strong to apprehend *and* grasp with all the saints [God's devoted people, the experience of that love] what is the breadth and length and height and depth [of it]; [that you might really come] to know the love of Christ, which far surpasses mere knowledge ...; that you may be filled [through all your being] unto all the fullness of God, **[may have the richest measure of the divine presence and become a body wholly filled and flooded with God Himself]**!' (Ephesians 3:18, 19, AMP).

We have this amazing privilege of carrying the glory of God on the earth, and His desire for us is that we will be more and more full of that glory, as we are increasingly transformed into His likeness. Now that is the awesome plan that He has for my life and yours, and nothing can thwart it, apart from my doubts and unbelief, because as long as I stay in faith and trust, He can and will use any and every circumstance to bring about that transformation. (See James 1:2-4.)

We recently quoted from Peter's letter that, 'His divine power has granted to us everything pertaining to life and Godliness, through the true knowledge of Him who called us by His own glory and excellence. For by these He has granted to us His precious and magnificent promises, so that by them you may become partakers of the divine nature...' (2 Peter 1:3, 4, NASB). And there it is again, you and I are destined to be partakers, or sharers of His divine nature, or carriers of His glory.

We have often shared in these reflections that, particularly when we are under pressure, giving thanks can help us to let that Christ life flow from deep within. In giving thanks we remind ourselves that the Holy Spirit is with us, and we can then cooperate with Him to produce His wonderful fruit in our lives. In addition, because it is His fruit, we will stay humbly walking with Him as we show forth His divine nature.

Often, when we have 'done well' in a situation, or when we have 'grown' and for example notice that we are much more patient or kind, or that we seem to be living with more peace or joy, we can find that that progress is challenged. Sometimes it feels like the enemy throws a curved ball and catches us out, and the accusation comes, 'So you haven't really changed at all'. Thanksgiving, I believe, will help us to demolish those discouraging accusations and help us not to give up, or slip back into old mindsets of trying harder to change ourselves instead of letting His life flow.

Our God is a God of increase, and He is changing me one degree at a time. That is sure and certain. Thanksgiving for this fact will help me, in those moments of discouragement, to stay in faith that God is at work in my life, that I am a new creation, and that He is growing my new nature daily as I walk with Him through all the ups and downs of everyday life. Thanksgiving is part of my faith declaration that I am moving from glory to glory by His Spirit, even if today I am feeling more aware of my shortcomings than victory.

Activation...

When we do see change, thanksgiving will seal our victories. When we have gained victory over a sin, a thought pattern or an unhelpful habit, giving thanks is like bolting the gate behind ourselves as we move on from one degree of glory to another. It's just part of celebrating who we now are in Christ, and who He is in us, so don't forget to celebrate those victories, give thanks, and enjoy the moment.

DAY 263 | Thanksgiving and Abiding

In that well known passage in John's Gospel, Jesus speaks of Himself as the vine and us as the branches. He lets us know that the key to bearing fruit is 'abiding' or 'remaining' in Him. He says, 'Abide in Me and I in you', and 'he who abides in Me and I in him, he bears much fruit ...' He says 'If you abide in Me, and My words abide in you, ask whatever you wish and it will be done for you.' He also tells them '... abide in My love.' (John 15:4, 5, 7, 9. NASB). In fact the whole passage closely links bearing fruit with i) 'abiding' in Him, ii) 'abiding' in His love and iii) letting His words abide in us.

The implications are clear, we are already 'in Him' we just have to stay there, in order to live fruitful lives, because if He is the vine then all the nourishment necessary for fruit bearing comes through Him. It's a simple picture from nature but very profound. The thing here is that it is not normal for a branch to disengage from the vine unless it is cut off, but once cut off it has no life of its own to survive, let alone carry any grapes to maturity.

The **normal thing is** for the branch to remain attached. We have a couple of vines in our garden and sure enough when we cut a branch off not only does the branch fail to produce grapes but within a day or two the leaves also die. To this day however we have never seen a branch detach itself; it just doesn't happen. Because the branches are integral to the whole vine, they grow and produce fruit quite naturally.

We have been thinking recently about how we can let 'our new life in Christ' flow in all sorts of different situations. Well here we have another key to help us. It is another picture that links to 'reckoning ourselves dead to sin and alive to God through Jesus.' In this picture it is about **recognising** (similar to reckoning) that on becoming a Christian we have been mystically repositioned, by the power of God 'into' Christ. We are now 'in Him' we just have to stay there. This can be very helpful in those times when we want to go on producing good fruit when 'the old me' wants to take over and react in the old ways.

Paul writes, 'For He has rescued us from the domain of darkness, and **transferred** us to the Kingdom of His beloved Son.' (Colossians 1:13,

NASB). We have been **'transferred'**, with a high price, into a new Kingdom. In footballing terms we no longer play for the old club any more. No one expects a player to go back and play for their old club after the transfer fee has been paid, and Paul emphasises this in his writing to another group of Christians by asking them, 'Do you not know that your body is the temple of the Holy Spirit, who is in you, whom you have received from God? You are not your own; **you were bought at a price**. Therefore honour God with your body.' (1 Corinthians 6:19,20).

The transfer fee was high; Jesus' own life, and we are now part of an entirely different Kingdom, we have no right to return to the old. The point I am making is that 'abiding' makes more sense and is easier to do, when we see how completely we have been repositioned. Abiding is not about 'trying' to stay connected to Jesus, it is about holding the position that we now have in Him. 'For you died, and your life is now hidden with Christ in God.' (Colossians 3:3).

The more that I can thank God that I have been 'transferred' and that I am now 'in Christ', the more faith I will have in my new position and the easier 'abiding' becomes. If I am no longer trying to see myself as 'in Christ' but 'reckon' on it as fact, the more I will appreciate and be able to appropriate all that He has done for me and all that is now available to me in Christ.

Activation . . .

Give thanks today that the price of the transfer has been paid, and let your thanksgiving release more and more faith that you are now 'in Christ'; that you can abide there, and that the 'vine life', His life will flow, producing fruit in all the different aspects of your life.

I think Paul would agree with me here, as he wrote, 'So then, just as you received Christ Jesus as Lord, continue to live in Him, rooted and built up in Him, strengthened in the faith as you were taught, **and overflowing with thankfulness**'. (Colossians 2:6).

DAY 264 | Thanksgiving and the Power of Words

One of the areas where we can struggle to fully live from our 'new man or woman in Christ' is in the area of our speech: those words that come out of our mouths, or in these days words typed on my phone, tablet or laptop released through social media. The Bible makes it clear that words are extremely important and have great power. 'The tongue has the power of life and death.' (Proverbs 18:21). Now this can be true literally, but for most of us it is mainly more true in terms of words that refresh, encourage or build up, as opposed to words that pull down, diminish or destroy.

James, in his discourse inspired by the Holy Spirit, is very clear about the power of words; the power of the tongue to bring life and build up, or bring death and destruction. (see James Chapter 3). Jesus also pointed out that our words are also very revealing about the state of our hearts, saying that it is "...out of the overflow of the heart the mouth speaks." (Matthew 12:34).

I had a dream the other night in which I was peering through a small hole in a wall, like a child, and on the other side was a beautiful garden, so green and so peaceful. I knew it was such a happy place. And the strong feeling I had was that this beautiful place was peaceful and happy because it was a place where no one was saying anything unkind, critical or judgmental about other people, nor were they thinking those sorts of thoughts about themselves. In the dream I wondered, 'how was that possible given the human condition?' The answer was that it was because the grace of God, the redemptive love of Jesus, and the overflowing life of the Spirit were dominant in all the lives of the people in that garden, and in all their conversations with each other, and with themselves.

By way of contrast the book of Revelation describes the devil as the accuser of the brethren, pointing out that he does it a lot – day and night – (Revelation 12:10). He uses his words to accuse us, and Jesus told us that "when he lies, he speaks his native language for he is a liar and the father of lies." (John 8:44). The devil quite clearly understands the power of words to destroy and I think he also incites us to accuse, or attack each other.

I have felt challenged recently to consider how easily and subtly we let ourselves off the hook in some of things we think and say about each other. It's interesting that many of the New Testament letters remind the readers to avoid, 'leave behind', or to stop gossiping, slandering, or malicious talk etc. (Colossians 3:8-10, 1 Timothy 3:11 & 5:13). Were the early Christians so bad, or are we being a bit too soft on ourselves?

By the way we are not saying we shouldn't be truthful with each other. As we have previously reflected, we need to encourage each other to leave behind stuff that belongs to the old self. And of course a genuinely loving, well motivated critique to improve something is not the same as being critical, as it is commonly understood. But we really don't want to cooperate with the devil by joining him in accusing each other in unkind ways.

Paul gives a clue as to how thanksgiving can really help in this journey to leave behind the words and conversations of the old self and to speak to each other as new men and women in Christ. He writes, 'Do not let any unwholesome talk come out of your mouths, but only what is helpful for building up others according to their needs, that it may benefit those who listen. And do not grieve the Holy Spirit of God, with whom you were sealed for the day of redemption.' (Ephesians 4:29). These words are then followed in chapter 5:4 by the need to replace unhealthy talking of all kinds **with thanksgiving.**

Activation . . .

Thanksgiving not only transforms how we speak to each other and ourselves, but it changes what is going on in our hearts at that deeper level. Then surprise, surprise, out of the overflow of our hearts our mouths speak, just as Jesus said. As you guard your mouth and what comes out of it with thanksgiving today, taste and see more of that place of joy, peace and healthy growth with others, and yourself, that I saw through the small hole in the fence in my dream.

DAY 265 | Thanksgiving and Focusing on the New Life in Christ

We can't leave this series of daily meditations (261-264) on our 'New Life in Christ' and 'Living from that New Christ life within', without taking a look at Eugene Peterson's thought provoking paraphrase of Romans 8:5-17 in The Message. He writes...

'Those who trust God's action in them find that God's Spirit is in them – living and breathing God! Obsession with self in these matters is a dead end; **attention to God leads us out into the open, into a spacious, free life.** Focusing on the self is the opposite of focusing on God. Anyone absorbed in self ignores God, ends up thinking more about self than God ... **But if God himself has taken up residence in your life, you can hardly be thinking more of yourself than of him.** Anyone, of course, who has not welcomed this invisible but clearly present God, the Spirit of Christ, won't know what we are talking about. But for you who welcome him, in whom He dwells- even though you still experience all the limitations of sin – you yourself experience life on God's terms. **It stands to reason doesn't it, that if the alive and present God who raised Jesus from the dead moves into your life, he'll do the same thing in you that he did in Jesus, bringing you alive to Himself? When God lives and breathes in you (and he does, as surely as he did in Jesus), you are delivered from that dead life. With His Spirit living in you, your body will be as alive as Christ's!***

So don't you see that we don't owe this old do-it-yourself life one red cent. There's nothing in it for us, nothing at all. The best thing is to give it a decent burial and **get on with your new life. God's Spirit beckons. There are things to do and places to go!**

This resurrection life you received from God is not a timid, grave-tending life. It's adventurously expectant, greeting God with a childlike "What's next, Papa?" God's Spirit touches our spirit and confirms who we really are.' (All the emphasis in bold is mine.)

The thing that resonates with me today is the emphasis that this paraphrase of this passage has on the need for us to focus on our New Life in Christ and not keep trying to deal with the old. It's a faith position that we take up here, as we have pointed out previously in several different ways. The old has gone the new has come, and what we focus on will become our reality.

The antidote to the 'obsession with self' that Eugene Patterson mentions here, is to stay grateful, and in thankfulness, for that New Life that we all now have deep within. Staying thankful for our 'New Life' is how we give the attention to God that leads us out into the 'open, spacious free life', that he describes. It is also worth noting here that the picture of the 'spacious' or 'broad' place is one that the psalmist uses (Psalms 18:19 & 36, and 31:8), to denote deliverance and freedom from his enemies.

This is such an incredible aspect of our salvation and one that accords with Jesus instruction to us to 'abide' in Him and let His words 'abide' in us, so that we bear much fruit. (John 15:4, 5, 7, 8). And I think that as we grasp the immensity of what He has done and is doing for us, our gratitude will move from 'making a willful choice' to give thanks, to just welling up and overflowing with gratitude from our hearts. (Matthew 12:34).

Activation...

Today, in any and every situation – the good, the bad and the ugly – give thanks to the Lord for His indwelling presence. It will keep your focus on Him and the empowering grace that comes as standard with His presence, and I believe that you will increasingly find yourself naturally producing good fruit that glorifies Jesus.

DAY 266 | Thanksgiving that helps us to 'lean'

Our thoughts today are inspired by the arrival here of a young man who has gone through many things in the past few years that have left him in need of 'time out' for rest and recuperation. As we have talked and he has shared his journey with us, we have been reminded again of the tender loving care of our heavenly Father, and the kindness that He showers upon us in our times of turmoil.

We have been struck by the fact that when we have been beaten up by the circumstances of life, the Lord does not always change those circumstances but walks with us 'through' them. 'Even though I walk through the valley of the shadow of death, I will fear no evil, for you are with me; your rod and staff they comfort me.' Or strengthen me. He even 'prepares a table before me in the presence of my enemies.' (Psalm 23:4, 5).

Sometimes, there are seasons in our life when there are shadows over us that just don't seem to shift. We pray and ask for deliverance, or wisdom, or a way out of that valley, but it just seems to go on and on. In these times more than any others it is important that we ask God, again, **who He is for us** in this particular situation and **what gift does He want to give us**.

Listening to this young man it became clear that the Lord was saying in answer to those (in this case unspoken) questions, firstly 'I am Emmanuel', the God who is with you. In other words this is not all happening because God has left you, or because you have done something wrong, or because you haven't had enough faith. The Lord silences all those accusing voices with those words, 'I am with you', or more emphatically, 'the I AM is with you'. Secondly in answer to the question, 'what gift do you have for me?' I believe the Lord would say, "the gift of being able to 'lean' on Me."

Walking through our valley's 'leaning' on the Lord is an incredible part of our heritage in Christ. We hear resonance of this in the Song of Songs 8:5, AMP. when the friends ask, "Who is this coming up from the wilderness leaning on her beloved?" Learning to let go and 'lean' on Him when we need to, in those seasons of life that are like a wilderness, works something in us that we may never fully understand here in this life. We just know that in these times our 'new life' in Christ can grow deeper and stronger. 'For our light and momentary troubles are achieving for us an eternal glory that far outweighs them all.' (2 Corinthians 4:17).

As we talked with this young man, it became clear that the key to being able to 'lean' in these times is all about 'yielding' to the Lord; about expressing our trust in Him by thanking Him that He is with us, that He will never leave or forsake us (Hebrews 13:5), and that He is with us to comfort us. As we do so, it keeps our hearts soft towards Him, and enables us to know, somewhere deep inside, that it's OK at this time to just 'lean'.

I am so grateful that in these times we don't just hear the harsh voice of a sergeant major, telling us to 'man up', but instead we hear again the invitation of our Heavenly Father through the words of Jesus, 'Come to me, all you who are weary and burdened, and I will give you rest.' (Matthew 11:28). He also reminds us here that He, the 'I Am', is gentle and humble in heart. And as we allow ourselves to 'just lean' we find that His refreshing, healing Spirit is at work in our spirit to renew and replenish us, and to lift our weariness... in His own good time.

Activation...

In those times of 'valley walking' thank the Lord that you can just lean on, or into, your wonderful Heavenly Fathers arms. He doesn't expect more of us than that intentional yielding and surrendering to His love and comfort. And then thank Him that it is in these times that your heart is ever more closely entwined with His.

DAY 267 | Thanksgiving that I am Surrounded

Yesterday we were reflecting on those times in our lives when we feel beaten up by the circumstances of life. We noted that the Lord does not always change those circumstances but walks through them with us. Sometimes, it can still seem as if the shadows over us just don't seem to shift. We pray and ask for deliverance, or wisdom, or a way out of the valley, but it just seems to go on and on with no immediate change. We can feel trapped, like someone in a besieged city, surrounded by an enemy.

Recently I was reading David's experience which he recounts for us in Psalms 31 and 32 and it would seem that this was how he felt too. 'Praise be to the Lord for he showed his wonderful love to me when I was in a besieged city. In my alarm I said, "I am cut off from your sight!" Yet you heard my cry for mercy when I called to you for help.' (31:21, 22). Then in Psalm 32 verse 7 we read, 'You are my hiding place; you will protect me from trouble and surround me with songs of deliverance.'

It is worth noting here that from the verses at the beginning of Psalm 32 we gather that this is the song of a forgiven man not a perfect one! We then get the declaration in verse 10 that reads, 'Many are the woes of the wicked, but the Lord's unfailing love surrounds the man (or woman) who trusts in Him.' This is a wonderful truth, with which you and I can fuel our thanksgiving because, not only is the Lord **with me** in the valley, (Psalm23:4), but in His love He Himself, **surrounds me there**.

In Psalm 31 verse 3 we have that very same truth expressed. 'Since you are my rock and fortress...' Inside this fortress he is surrounded by the Lord's 'thick walls'. Other scriptures also emphasise that we are surrounded by the Lord and His love; protected and safe, even when our circumstances and feelings suggest that we are under siege, or surrounded by troubles. 'For in the day of trouble He will keep me safe in His dwelling; He will hide me in the shelter of His tabernacle and set me high upon a rock.' (Psalm 27:5). 'The angel of the Lord encamps around those who fear Him, and he delivers them.' (Psalm 34:7). 'The name of the Lord is a strong tower; the righteous run into it and are safe.' (Proverbs 18:10).

In our times of difficulty however, we often don't 'see it'. So let's have a look at what happened for Elisha's servant in the city of Dothan. The servant gets up (to make Elisha's morning cup of tea?!) and he sees the city is surrounded by horses and chariots. 'A very strong force'. Understandably he panics. The enemy king is not friendly, in fact he is 'enraged', so the servant tells Elisha, who simply says. "Don't be afraid." (2 Kings 6:11-20).

Now at this point, (let's admit it!) some of us might have got angry – like when our well meaning Christian friends tell us 'not to worry' about something that is making us very anxious. "Be realistic" we cry, "It's bad". And it certainly looked bad for Elisha and his servant. But like the servant we often forget one thing: Elisha, like Jesus, always adds the big BECAUSE when He tells us not to be anxious. Jesus doesn't just pat us on the shoulder, saying "don't be anxious, it will be fine." He says 'Don't be anxious BECAUSE your heavenly Father knows what you need, (Matthew 6:25-32), and you are very, very valuable to Him, (Matthew 10:29-31). Likewise Elisha said in effect "Don't be afraid, BECAUSE there is an even larger army with us."

Elisha then prays that his servant's eyes will be opened. He then sees that the hills around them are full of horses and chariots of fire. Wow. Please notice 'full' and 'fire'! You and I need our eyes opened to see just how powerfully we are surrounded by the Lord, His love, His power and His angelic forces. And so this is where thanksgiving can really help us. The more we thank the Lord for these truths, the more our eyes will be opened to the full reality of our situation. Then our faith will rise to see that we are surrounded by the Lord, His love, His resources and His power, even in our dark valleys.

Activation ...

Thanksgiving opens our eyes to the BECAUSE of God and, when I begin to see the truths behind the BECAUSE more clearly, 'songs of deliverance' and thanksgiving will ignite in my heart and flow from my lips. "It may look like I'm surrounded, but I'm surrounded by You." (Have a listen to Michael W Smith https://youtu.be/YBl84oZxnJ4) You may then find that thanksgiving itself becomes a major way in which you fight your battles.

DAY 268 | Thanksgiving for His Wrap-around Love and Care

When the Israelites were travelling through the wilderness, they had a most amazing visual aid of God's surrounding presence. God made sure that they knew He was with them. 'By day the Lord went ahead of them in a pillar of cloud to guide them on their way and by night in a pillar of fire to give them light, so that they could travel by day or night. Neither the pillar of cloud by day nor the pillar of fire by night left its place in front of the people.' (Exodus 13:21, 22). When they needed guidance and direction, there was the manifest presence of the Lord ahead of them, leading them onwards.

When they reached the Red Sea, and they couldn't go forward, they panicked, (and who wouldn't?) because the Egyptian army was closing in on them from behind. We then see an even more vivid picture of the Lord's protection of His people. 'Then the angel of God, who had been travelling in front of Israel's army, withdrew and went behind them. The pillar of cloud also moved from in front and stood behind them, coming between the armies of Egypt and Israel. Throughout the night the cloud brought darkness to the one side and light to the other; so that neither went near the other all night long.' (Exodus 14:19, 20). Now – when they needed it – the manifest presence of God was protecting them from behind.

They had to grow in faith and trust that God would be there all through that night and that somehow, trapped as they were, God was going to make a way for them where there was no way. They maybe hoped the Egyptians would get tired and go home, or that the angel of the Lord in the fiery pillar would chase them away, or even go through the Egyptian camp and burn it up. Whatever hope they had, they could not possibly have imagined what was going to happen next.

We, of course, can because we've probably seen it on film with CGI, but take a step back and imagine what it was like. Nothing could have prepared them for this. As Moses stretched out his hand, 'the Lord drove the sea back with a strong east wind and turned it into dry land. The waters were divided, and the Israelites went through the sea on dry ground, with a wall of water on their right and on their left.' (Exodus 14:21, 22).

The Lord makes a way to give them safe passage away from their enemies. He opens a way in front, hides them from behind, and He even provided them with a wall on each side. A wall of water that collapsed in onto the Egyptian army when they tried to follow. It is no wonder that Miriam, Moses' sister and a prophetess, took hold of her tambourine and led the dancing as they all sang their songs of deliverance. (Exodus 15:20). The Lord goes before them, behind them and protects them on both sides too. I think that is called 'all round protection'. They feel as if they are surrounded by enemies, but they are surrounded by Him.

I, in my lifetime, have never seen that kind of physical manifestation of the Lord surrounding me with His protection, but we are called to 'walk by faith and not by sight.' (2 Corinthians 5:7, NASB). And I know that there have been many deliverances in my life, those I have been aware of and those, many I believe, that I have been unaware of; protection that the Lord, in His graciousness, has provided.

Looking at Psalm 62:2 in The Passion Translation we read, 'He alone is my safe place; his wrap-around presence always protects me. For he is my champion defender; there's no risk of failure with God.' And in verse 7 we read, 'God's glory is all around me! His wrap-around presence is all I need, for the Lord is my Saviour, my hero, and my life giving strength.'

Activation...

So how do we 'walk by faith' and not by sight in these things? How do we live trusting in the Lord's 'wrap-around' twenty four seven care for us? I believe it is as we glean from His word the truth about who He is and who He wants to be for His people, and we thank Him for it. And, as we thank Him, I believe our 'spiritual eyes' will be opened to 'see' His hand in our lives, and so, like David, we will be praising Him for our own daily deliverances, for He 'daily bears our burdens'. He is for us a 'God of deliverances;' (Psalm 68:19, 20, NASB).

DAY 269 | Thanksgiving and Peace

Not so long ago I was chatting with a friend who was going through a difficult time. He said that the thing he most longed for was peace. He felt that he could do anything, even difficult things if he had peace. The trouble was that he was not happy with the way the Lord (and others) were managing the situation in which he found himself, and this was affecting His trust in God's good hand in his life and situation. He knew with his head that the Lord is good and to be trusted, but his feelings were at odds with his head! And he didn't have peace.

In this context I was very impressed reading 2 Peter 1:2 'Grace and peace be yours in abundance through the knowledge of God and our Lord Jesus Christ'. The **'through'** strikes me strongly. Peace and Grace don't regularly come on us like dollops of cream from God, in some sort of dissociated way, they come **through** our knowledge of Him. That knowledge is a combination of knowledge of the truth of His word, His character, and an experiential relationship with Him. The word 'knowledge' in the bible often carries with it an implication of intimate relationship. (Genesis 4:1, Matthew 1:25, AV).

I think that we often forget that, and so we may pray, "Give me peace Lord", rather like someone may say to their doctor, "Give me some valium doc." Now valium can work, anxiety may fade and you feel more peaceful – for a while – until it wears off. Likewise God in His grace, like the tender shepherd He is, does give us peace when we cry out to Him, even at times when we are not in the greatest place with Him. But it probably won't last if we don't reconnect with Him by faith in spirit (in relationship and intimacy) and truth (His promises, word and character).

Surely this is the power of Jesus' promise in Matthew 11:28-30, "Come to me, all you who are weary and burdened, and I will give you rest" "Yes Lord" we say "your rest and peace, thank you". But we may miss the "Come unto me." Just as in Peter's letter, the rest and peace is closely linked to relationship. "Come and be close." says Jesus. But there is more, and in verses 29 and 30, Jesus is saying, "if you want **ongoing** rest and peace for your souls you need to stay close "take my yoke upon you" , stay connected. And even more "learn from me", stay close, listen, respond and be changed.

Lasting, ongoing peace can't be divorced from being, staying and growing close to the Lord Jesus in spirit and in truth. So, back to 2 Peter 1:3, 'His divine power has given us everything (including peace) we need for life and godliness **through** our knowledge of Him who called us by His own glory and goodness.' There it is again, everything we need including peace comes '**through**' our knowledge of Him; knowledge of the truth in His word, His promises and His character in our 'un-peaceful' situation. It is peace both in life – the practical things, and in godliness – my spiritual journey with its challenges and battles.

In Romans 15:13 Paul prays 'May the God of hope fill you with all joy and peace as you trust in Him, (in believing – NASB), so that you may overflow with hope by the power of the Holy Spirit.' 'All joy and peace' sounds exactly what I need in life. And 'the power of the Holy Spirit' is a big factor in that, since joy and peace are both fruit of the Holy Spirit. The 'joy and the peace' come, according to Paul, 'as you trust in Him' or 'in believing'. There we go! Once again we are reminded that faith and trust are vital if we are to receive peace and live in peace, in an ongoing way.

Some days faith can feel nebulous, hard to grasp, and too spiritual to grip onto, especially in the hard times and in adverse circumstances. But, as we have realised again and again over this year, thanksgiving is one of the best, the most powerful and the most effective ways of growing in faith. And it is a very available and practical way to feed faith. Thanksgiving is 'easy' in the sense that it is a clear choice, I just need to decide to do it, regardless of feelings and circumstances.

Activation . . .

Paul exhorted his friends in Philippi to 'Rejoice in the Lord', (Philippians 3:1), several times, 'again I say rejoice' (Phil 4:4), closely followed by 'thanksgiving' (verse 6) and then peace (verse 7). It is a solid piece of advice and, as you rejoice, things start to change on the inside, knowledge of the truth dawns afresh, faith begins to rise, we sense the love of the Lord Jesus again, and by the power of the Spirit, joy and peace fill me afresh.

DAY 270 | Thanksgiving and our Life Together in Christ

One of the main ways in which we, Christ's body on earth, are called to validate our claim that He is the Saviour of the world, is by the way we do life together as His people. Jesus' Last Supper discourse with His disciples, and prayer for them, recorded for us in John chapters 13-17, show us that this was the plan. At this precious time, when Jesus knew that He was soon to leave them, He repeatedly spoke about the love that was to be between them, and between all who would believe in Him from that time on. So let's listen in again to Jesus, as He spoke to those disciples saying, "A new command I give you: Love one another. As I have loved you, so you must love one another. By this all men will know that you are my disciples, if you love one another." (John 13:34). "Whoever has my commands and obeys them, he is the one who loves me. He who loves me will be loved by my Father, and I too will love Him and show myself to him". (John 14: 21). "My command is this: Love each other as I have loved you." (John 15:12).

And let's also listen to Jesus' conversation with His father. "Holy Father, protect them by the power of your name – the name you gave me – so that they may be one as we are one." (John 17:11). "My prayer is not for them alone. I pray for all those who will believe in me through their message, that all of them may be one, Father, just as you are in me and I am in you. **May they also be in us so that the world may believe that you have sent me. I have given them the glory that you gave me, that they may be one as we are one: I in them and you in me. May they be brought to complete unity to let the world know that you have sent me and have loved them even as you have loved me."** (John 17:20-23).

Unity and oneness are to be the hallmarks of our life together as Christians. Not only does this bring glory to God and point the world to the authenticity of the gospel, it also delights the Father's heart and causes Him to dwell more evidently with us in our communities. (See Psalm 133). However, like Mary we can find ourselves (if we are honest) wondering "How can these things be?" The answer, I think, is to be found in that wonderful, but sometimes overlooked, phrase '**I have given them the glory that you gave me,** that they may be one as we are one'. This love and unity is, and always will be, a complete miracle, brought about by the power of God, through Christ, indwelling each one of us.

If at any time you have been in a meeting or spent time with the Lord and felt His blessing, you will be aware of a greater love for your brothers and sisters in your heart. In reality we can only love as His love and glory rests upon us day by day. And what does His glory look or feel like? Well let us stand next to Moses as he asks the Lord to reveal His glory to him. 'And the Lord said "I will cause all my goodness to pass in front of you and I will proclaim my name (character)." And 'then the Lord came down in the cloud..., proclaiming, "The Lord, the Lord, the compassionate and gracious God, slow to anger, abounding in love and faithfulness, maintaining love to thousands, and forgiving wickedness..."' (Exodus 33:19 & 34:5, 6, 7).

It would seem that God's glory is completely entwined in His character; it's who He in essence is. And as He gives His glory to those of us now 'in Christ', those qualities will be found in us. He has loved us enough to save us and given us a new nature, so that same love amongst us becomes possible. We too can now be 'compassionate, gracious, slow to anger and abounding in love and faithfulness', as we allow the Holy Spirit to live in and through us.

John, the apostle of love writes, 'We love because He first loved us.' 'God is love' he tells us so, 'Whoever lives in love lives in God and God in him... Whoever loves God must also love his brother.' (1 John 4:16-19). For John there is no alternative lifestyle but we, of course, still have that choice to 'live by the Spirit' by reckoning ourselves 'dead to our old life and alive to Christ', or to go on living according to our old sinful nature.

Let Paul's words be your encouragement to make the right choice in each moment. 'Therefore, as God's chosen people, holy and dearly loved, clothe yourselves with compassion, kindness, humility, gentleness and patience. Bear with each other and forgive whatever grievances you may have... Forgive as the Lord forgave you. And over all these virtues put on love, which binds them all together in perfect unity. Let the peace of Christ rule in your hearts... **and be thankful.**' (Colossians 3:12-15).

DAY 271 | Thanksgiving and Joy

Over the past couple of days we have written about peace and love as hallmarks of our life in Christ. Both of those grace gifts come from the Holy Spirit, our indwelling helper. They are of course 'fruits' of the Spirit that grow in us as we allow His life to flow through us, carrying the nourishment that produces the fruit in our lives, like the grapes on the branches of a vine.

In the natural world the sap carrying that nourishment in any particular plant doesn't make just any fruit, but the fruit that is of the kind that that particular plant was created for. 'Then God said, "Let the land produce vegetation; seed-bearing plants and trees on the land that bear fruit with seed in it, according to their various kinds." And it was so.' (Genesis 1:11).

We too will produce fruit, as the Holy Spirit flows through us with all His grace, help and encouragement, according to 'our kind'. That is to say, according to our new 'life in Christ'. We can now expect to produce Christ like fruit as He flows through our unique personality. This is why Paul could encourage the Galatian Christians to expect, if they 'lived by the Spirit', that they would produce a lot of good fruit. (Galatians 5:16, 22-26).

Like the other fruit – 'Peace' and 'Love' etc – 'Joy' originates in the heart of our Creator God. The Old Testament is full of prophetic encouragements to God's people to rejoice and be full of joy at His deliverances and His work on their behalf, even promising them 'everlasting joy'. (Isaiah 61:7). The Jews were often encouraged to celebrate and have days of 'feasting and joy'. (Esther 9:22). And of course we know that God Himself rejoices over His people with 'great joy'. (Zephaniah 3:17).

Speaking of Jesus, the writer to the Hebrews said of Him, "God, your God, has set you above your companions by anointing you with the oil of joy." (Hebrews 1:9). And we know that even in the darkest of all days for Jesus, He chose the cross, 'for the joy set before Him' (Hebrews 12:2). The joy that is echoed in heaven over each one of us who have repented and fully turned to Jesus. (Luke 15:7).

Joy is in the heart of God, heaven is full of it, and God fully intends to share His joy with us. Reading through both the Old and New Testament we can see that it is a very high priority in His Kingdom. So much so, in fact, that the Holy Spirit inspired Paul to write that, 'The Kingdom of God ... is righteousness, peace and joy in the Holy Spirit...' (Romans 14:17).

Righteousness and peace we understand; no one can enter the Kingdom without the **righteousness** of Christ, which brings us to a place of **peace** with God. The '**joy**' aspect, which I think is probably very unique to Christianity, is less explainable. It feels like it just bursts from God's heart because His plan has worked. We are now His and He is ours in such a unique and special way. His plan has worked! Jesus has got His 'Bride'!

This is why I believe our 'joy' and 'rejoicing' will always be, not just in what He does for us while we are here on earth, but primarily in our restored relationship with Him. This is why our thanksgiving needs to move beyond thanking Him for His gifts to us, and what He does for us, to thanksgiving that we have this incredible relationship with Him, the King of all Kings, our Creator and Saviour. We are **THE** most privileged people in the whole of the earth. We have our heavenly 'Bridegroom' to love and care for us.

Activation...

Thank Him today afresh for the privilege, and the wonder of being called into such a high calling. Let that thanksgiving lead you to 'exult and thrill with inexpressible and glorious (triumphant and heavenly) joy.' (1 Peter 1:8, AMP).

DAY 272 | Thanksgiving, His Joy and Ours

Yesterday we were considering the 'joy' that is in the Godhead, over us!!! Over us His people, The 'Bride of Christ'. We also looked at our 'joy' in the Lord, in the wonder, that the King of all Kings 'should die to save a wretch like me'. (William How).

For most of us that joy is tempered by the fact that, like the Shulammite in the Song of Songs, we find it very hard to believe that we really are that acceptable to God, or that He can in fact delight in us. Apart from the fact that it sounds rather proud, we are often all too aware of our faults and failings to be really relaxed in our relationship with the Almighty.

So today our thanksgiving revolves around the wonderful truth that the Lord has a totally different perspective to ours. In spite of being totally holy and pure Himself, a Being who cannot even look upon sin, He comes, by His Spirit, to live in us, to walk beside us and, yes, to even enjoy us. Now for most of us that takes some believing, and yet this is exactly what the Lord wants for His people in this day. He is wanting us to grasp this truth as a source of incredible joy. It's a 'truth' that will alter the way we see ourselves and that too will give us, and God, even more joy. (Zephaniah 3:17).

The main point is that the Lord has not just saved us to go into an earthly remand home until we have sorted our lives out to a sufficient enough degree, so that we can go to heaven. He has saved us, made us alive with Christ and raised us up with Him to be seated in the heavenly realm... 'in Christ Jesus'. (Ephesians 2:6). Seated **'with Him'**. This is a total mystery, we have been sanctified and yet we are being sanctified daily. You and I are 'saints', that is how He sees us now, and yet still by His grace, and the work of the indwelling Spirit, He is continually changing us to be more and more like Jesus. (2 Corinthians 3:18).

We are now totally loved by our triune God. How do we know? Jesus laid down His life for us and specifically said that there is no greater love than that. (John 15:13). He also said, "I have loved you, [just] as the Father has loved Me..." (John 15:9, AMP). We are now also recipients of the same love from the heart of the Father that Jesus has. Amazing or what? But Jesus said it in His prayer to His Father, "... may they be brought to complete unity to let the world may know (Father) that you sent me and have loved them even as you have loved me." (John 17: 23). Then there is the Holy Spirit. Well He certainly loves us. Love is one of His fruits and letting us know how much God loves us is one of His main delights. (Romans 5:5).

This then is the 'unconditional love' that you and I long for, and it is all because our lives are now '... hidden with Christ in God', (Colossians 3:3). I for one can't quite get my head around this, so I thought I would share with you the words from a poem, by Jonathan Bugden. So today, as you read over the scriptures I have quoted above, and read this poem, give Him your thanks for His incredible love, and as you do let the reality of it fill your mind, and let your heart swell with the joy that this truth brings.

Romanced by the Three.

Entwined and encircled, I'm loved by the three.
It's hard to imagine why they want this with me,
But the love I encounter is deeper than sea,
Beyond comprehension, yet given to me
is the love and embrace of the Eternal Three.

Blissfully lost in a dance with the Three,
I'm wonderfully held, yet utterly free,
There's mystery and certainty found in their eyes
That baffles all logic and reason defies.
I'm lost in a love that's the gift of the Three.

A tsunami of mercy that streams from the three,
With relentless compassion for all that they see,
Restoring connection, reopening doors,
To their love and delight and their passion for more,
That's the life in the Eternal Three.

Peace, joy and wisdom reside in the Three,
But gladly and freely they're offered to me.
That lifts me above the noise of my life,
Altering perception of struggle strife
I can powerfully soar in the arms of the Three.[1]

DAY 273 | Thanksgiving for a God who Gives

When we began this year of thanksgiving, I had no idea how absolutely fundamental, and essential, thanksgiving was going to prove to be in our relationship with the Lord. We started with Psalm 100:4 *'Enter his gates with thanksgiving and his courts with praise; give thanks to him and praise His name. For the Lord is good and His love endures forever; his faithfulness continues through all generations.'*

We recognised thanksgiving as a key to 'entering His gates', to coming together into His presence when we meet with others, or on our own. As we have journeyed through the last eight months, however, it has become more and more clear that 'Thanksgiving' needs to be integral to every part of our life in Christ, and during the night, I felt that the Lord revealed another profound reason why we can gladly follow Paul's encouragement to, 'Be joyful always; pray continually; **give thanks in all circumstances**, for this is God's will for you in Christ Jesus.' (1 Thessalonians 5:16-18.)

The reason He gave was simply this: We as a people, should be hallmarked by gratitude because we have a '**Giving** God', a God who delights to **give**, who in fact ceaselessly looks for opportunity to pour out blessing and favour on His people. The relationship between us and God, is based on the fact that He is a generous **giver**, and we are His beneficiaries. In James 1:5, for example, we are encouraged to ask God for wisdom if we need it. The literal translation of the Greek phrase is, 'ask from the **giving** God to all men unreservedly and not reproaching and it will be given...' That's our God!

Let us not take any of this for granted, because so many of the other 'gods' in the world are demanding. Do this! Don't do that! Follow these rules! Obey these edicts etc. So many religions are founded on rules to either appease their god, or earn favour. Even the secular 'gods', like money and fame, extort a high price from those who worship them. Our God – Father, Son, and Holy Spirit – are **givers**; all of them. And so we, God's people, thrive as we receive forgiveness, love, blessings, help, strength, wisdom, and on and on – the list is endless.

Most of us will know the gospel verse, 'For God so loved the world that He *'gave'* His one and only Son, that whoever believes on Him shall not perish but have eternal life', but phew!! what a mind blower that really is when you stop and think. God so loved that He *gave*. Jesus too didn't have to *give* His life, but He wanted to, and He did, because of love for you and me. (John 3:16). And it cost Him greatly. John writes at the beginning of his Gospel, 'to all who received him, to those who believed in his name, he *gave* (there's that word again) the right to become children of God.' We didn't earn it, He *gave* it to us, and so, 'From the fullness of His grace we have all received one blessing after another.' (John 1:12 & 16). All freely *given*. Now that is good news!

The more we catch sight of the bigness of God's heart towards us, the more we will become continual, daily 'receivers' of all His grace, mercy, forgiveness, love, kindness, and help. Consider this, 'He who did not spare his own Son, but *gave* him up for us all – how will he not also along with him, graciously *give* us all things?' (Romans 8:32). As we become aware of God's great generosity towards us, we will find ourselves becoming continuously thankful, in everything, and for all things.

Activation . . .

Today consider this:- The Father has *given* us His Son. He has drawn us into His family, *giving* us our new identity as 'a child of God'. He loves, sustains, protects and provides for us; just a few of the things He freely *gives*.

Jesus freely *gave* His life for us, (Have a slow read of Isaiah 53), providing us with salvation, forgiveness, acceptance, entrance into the family of God, and then He *gives* us a new life and the grace to grow into His likeness.

The Holy Spirit takes all that the Father and Son have for us, bringing it gladly into our lives, *giving* us His help, counsel, friendship, leading, teaching and transforming power. (John 14:15, 16 & 26, AMP), (John16:13-15).

In fact 'His divine power has *given* us everything that we need for life and godliness through our knowledge of him who has called us by his own glory and goodness.' (2 Peter 1:3) All is indeed ours as *gifts* from the three, and so this is why gratitude is the only response that we can have.

DAY 274 | 'Giving Thanks' is giving a gift

As we reflected yesterday on the truth that our God is a giver through and through our hearts were thrilled again to recognise that God is love, and that His love is directed without measure towards us, His children. Sometimes our concept and ideas about love are clouded by the modern expressions of love that seem to be more about what I can get from others, than what I can give. 1 Corinthians 13, the famous chapter on love, brings us back to an understanding that love is outward looking and outward focused onto those who are the objects of its love. Love gives and gives again. So the truths that God is love, and that God is the universe's greatest giver, unquestionably hang together.

Today let's build on the thrill of being reminded of these truths about our God, and let us consider how that affects us and who we are in this 'dance' with the Trinity by looking at the word on which these books are based; the word 'Thanksgiving'. Thanksgiving is giving thanks. Obvious? –Yes! But think about it, at the heart of giving thanks is the choice to **give** something, to be like our Heavenly Father. So let's unpack that a little more!

Firstly if I freely give something it means *it's a gift*. Getting something that I have paid for, like a new washing machine, is not a gift. The wages you receive from work are not a gift. A gift is freely given, it cannot be forced out of you, legally demanded from you, or be part of a binding transaction. Jesus said, 'Freely have you received, freely give.' (Matthew 10:8).This is such a good reminder for us because as we travel on the road as Christians it is easy to get bogged down in what I ought to be doing as a good Christian and to lose the joy and freedom of wanting to express myself by giving freely. Could this have been part of the loss of first love by the Christians in Ephesus? (Revelation 2:4).

Secondly *giving a gift* is an expression of love. After nine months of reflecting on all sorts of aspects of thanksgiving, let us meditate on the fact that whenever I freely give something I am expressing love. So when I move in thanksgiving, I am expressing my love to the Lord. I am loving Him, and showing my love for Him. It can feel good and right to express your love and affection for people in your family and your world. How much more so with the Lord. Allow yourself the pleasure of expressing your love to Jesus by giving Him the gift of thanks. 'Thank you for dying for me, for taking all my sin, guilt and shame, all of it'. 'Thank you for a clean conscience'. 'Thank you for life, health, food, friends, family and so much more.'

Thirdly *a gift involves a choice*. I don't have to give a gift of flowers to someone, but I can choose to. I don't have to thank Jesus for a cleansed conscience and for peace, but I can choose to. Choice makes the gift all the more special. When you, or I, choose thanksgiving we give the Lord something special. Sometimes when we give a gift and the person is pleased we say, "Oh it was nothing really". We are wrong. It was something; it was a choice, an act of love, a gift, and so it is when we give to the Lord. Let your heart expand with that realisation, and consider Jesus' response to the one leper in ten who chose to come back to give Him thanks. (Luke 17:15-19).

And fourthly, to expand your heart even more, think on – *who am I giving my gift of thanksgiving to?* Father, Son and Holy Spirit! Well isn't that marvelous? You and I have the power to shower gifts on Father, Son and Holy Spirit. They need nothing, being fully complete in themselves, yet we have the power, in giving thanks, to shower them with gifts on a daily basis. Of course any and every gift of thanks we give them is more than fully, richly deserved, and only scratches the surface of what we have to thank them for. There is so much more to be grateful for than we are aware of, or indeed would even have time to say; nevertheless isn't it wonderful that we can imitate our giving God and be 'givers' ourselves by showering Him with our gifts of gratitude?

Activation...

As you come to the end of this book, ask the Lord to increase your appreciation of all that He has **given** you and **gives** you daily, and so continue to grow in gratitude, day by day, with the Holy Spirit's help. Think some more today about the power and value of your thanksgiving in the heavenly realm. Sense the delight in Father, Son and Holy Spirit as you **give** them your thanks today, and determine to continue this journey of 'Thanksgiving'.

What next?

As before, we pray that, as you have read and pondered these daily devotionals, you have absorbed some more of the relentless love that God has for you, and that you have been drawn closer to Him day by day.

For some the four books may take you through a year, others may find it more helpful to travel through the books more slowly, taking longer.

I believe there will be lasting benefit in reading through all four books in a regular rhythm, at the pace that suits you best, we are all different.

We are planning to publish Book Four in the late autumn.

If you would like to purchase Book Four, further copies of Book Three, or of Books One and Two, then please email us at:-

enquiries@lifetraining.co.uk.

Notes

Day 193
1. Jonathan Bugden. Romanced by the Three. Recorded by David Hadden on 'Heaven Sings' © 2021 Sounds of Wonder

Day 205
1. Keith Green. Oh Lord You're Beautiful. © Copyright 1980 Birdwing music/BMG Songs Inc/EMI Christian Music Publishing

Day 225
1. Rev. Willis Judson Beecher, Professor of Hebrew language and literature. The Prophets and the Promise. p 314 © Copyright 1905 by Beecher, Thomas W Cromwell & co.
2. Bob Mumford. Stepping Over the Threshold. © 2020 Lifechangers

Day 234
1. Arthur Burke and Sylvia Gunter. Blessing your Spirit © Copyright 2005 The Father's Business.

Day 237
1. Bob Mumford. Stepping Over the Threshold. © 2020 Lifechangers

Day 239
1. C S Lewis. The Lion the Witch and the Wardrobe. 1950 Geoffrey Bles Ltd.

Day 260
1. Graham Cooke The Newness Advantage. Chapter 5. © Brilliant Book House. 2017

Day 272
1. Jonathan Bugden. Romanced by the Three